OPPOSING
VIEWPOINTS®
SERIES

Judicial Activism

Other Books of Related Interest:

Opposing Viewpoints Series

Church and State

Democracy

Election Spending

Illegal Immigration

At Issue Series

The Ethics of Capital Punishment

Health Care Legislation

Should Juveniles Be Given Life Without Parole?

Should Religious Symbols Be Used on Public Land?

Current Controversies Series

Gays in the Military

Government Corruption

Politics and the Media

The Tea Party Movement

"Congress shall make no law ... abridging the freedom of speech, or of the press."

First Amendment to the US Constitution

The basic foundation of our democracy is the First Amendment guarantee of freedom of expression. The *Opposing Viewpoints* series is dedicated to the concept of this basic freedom and the idea that it is more important to practice it than to enshrine it.

Judicial Activism

Noah Berlatsky, Book Editor

GREENHAVEN PRESS
A part of Gale, Cengage Learning

Detroit • New York • San Francisco • New Haven, Conn • Waterville, Maine • London

GALE
CENGAGE Learning®

Elizabeth Des Chenes, *Managing Editor*

© 2012 Greenhaven Press, a part of Gale, Cengage Learning.

Gale and Greenhaven Press are registered trademarks used herein under license.

For more information, contact:
Greenhaven Press
27500 Drake Rd.
Farmington Hills, MI 48331-3535
Or you can visit our Internet site at gale.cengage.com

For product information and technology assistance, contact us at

Gale Customer Support, 1-800-877-4253
For permission to use material from this text or product, submit all requests online at
www.cengage.com/permissions

Further permissions questions can be emailed to permissionrequest@cengage.com

Articles in Greenhaven Press anthologies are often edited for length to meet page requirements. In addition, original titles of these works are changed to clearly present the main thesis and to explicitly indicate the author's opinion. Every effort is made to ensure that Greenhaven Press accurately reflects the original intent of the authors. Every effort has been made to trace the owners of copyrighted material.

Cover Image copyright trekandshoot/Shutterstock.com.

LIBRARY OF CONGRESS CATALOGING-IN-PUBLICATION DATA

Judicial activism / Noah Berlatsky.
    p. cm. -- (Opposing viewpoints) Summary: "Judicial Activism: Is Judicial Activism Harmful?; How Has Judicial Activism Affected Particular Issues?; What Is the Relationship Between Public Opinion and Judicial Activism?; Is Judicial Activism an Issue in Other Countries?"-- Provided by publisher.
    Includes bibliographical references and index.
    ISBN 978-0-7377-5729-3 (hardback) -- ISBN 978-0-7377-5730-9 (paperback)
    1. Political questions and judicial power--United States. 2. Political questions and judicial power. I. Berlatsky, Noah.
    KF5130.J83 2011
    347.73'12--dc22
                                                            2011011651

Printed in the United States of America
1 2 3 4 5 6 7 15 14 13 12 11

Contents

Chapter 3: What Is the Relationship Between Public Opinion and Judicial Activism?

Chapter 4: Is Judicial Activism an Issue in Other Countries?

Why Consider Opposing Viewpoints?

> *"The only way in which a human being can make some approach to knowing the whole of a subject is by hearing what can be said about it by persons of every variety of opinion and studying all modes in which it can be looked at by every character of mind. No wise man ever acquired his wisdom in any mode but this."*
>
> John Stuart Mill

In our media-intensive culture it is not difficult to find differing opinions. Thousands of newspapers and magazines and dozens of radio and television talk shows resound with differing points of view. The difficulty lies in deciding which opinion to agree with and which "experts" seem the most credible. The more inundated we become with differing opinions and claims, the more essential it is to hone critical reading and thinking skills to evaluate these ideas. Opposing Viewpoints books address this problem directly by presenting stimulating debates that can be used to enhance and teach these skills. The varied opinions contained in each book examine many different aspects of a single issue. While examining these conveniently edited opposing views, readers can develop critical thinking skills such as the ability to compare and contrast authors' credibility, facts, argumentation styles, use of persuasive techniques, and other stylistic tools. In short, the Opposing Viewpoints Series is an ideal way to attain the higher-level thinking and reading skills so essential in a culture of diverse and contradictory opinions.

In addition to providing a tool for critical thinking, *Opposing Viewpoints* books challenge readers to question their own strongly held opinions and assumptions. Most people form their opinions on the basis of upbringing, peer pressure, and personal, cultural, or professional bias. By reading carefully balanced opposing views, readers must directly confront new ideas as well as the opinions of those with whom they disagree. This is not to simplistically argue that everyone who reads opposing views will—or should—change his or her opinion. Instead, the series enhances readers' understanding of their own views by encouraging confrontation with opposing ideas. Careful examination of others' views can lead to the readers' understanding of the logical inconsistencies in their own opinions, perspective on why they hold an opinion, and the consideration of the possibility that their opinion requires further evaluation.

Evaluating Other Opinions

To ensure that this type of examination occurs, *Opposing Viewpoints* books present all types of opinions. Prominent spokespeople on different sides of each issue as well as well-known professionals from many disciplines challenge the reader. An additional goal of the series is to provide a forum for other, less known, or even unpopular viewpoints. The opinion of an ordinary person who has had to make the decision to cut off life support from a terminally ill relative, for example, may be just as valuable and provide just as much insight as a medical ethicist's professional opinion. The editors have two additional purposes in including these less known views. One, the editors encourage readers to respect others' opinions—even when not enhanced by professional credibility. It is only by reading or listening to and objectively evaluating others' ideas that one can determine whether they are worthy of consideration. Two, the inclusion of such viewpoints encourages the important critical thinking skill of objectively evaluating an author's credentials and bias. This evaluation will illuminate an author's reasons for taking a particular stance on an issue and will aid in readers' evaluation of the author's ideas.

It is our hope that these books will give readers a deeper understanding of the issues debated and an appreciation of the complexity of even seemingly simple issues when good and honest people disagree. This awareness is particularly important in a democratic society such as ours in which people enter into public debate to determine the common good. Those with whom one disagrees should not be regarded as enemies but rather as people whose views deserve careful examination and may shed light on one's own.

Thomas Jefferson once said that "difference of opinion leads to inquiry, and inquiry to truth." Jefferson, a broadly educated man, argued that "if a nation expects to be ignorant and free . . . it expects what never was and never will be." As individuals and as a nation, it is imperative that we consider the opinions of others and examine them with skill and discernment. The *Opposing Viewpoints* series is intended to help readers achieve this goal.

David L. Bender and Bruno Leone,
Founders

Introduction

Perhaps the most controversial political battle involving judicial activism occurred in 1937. Democrat Franklin D. Roosevelt (FDR) had been reelected president in 1936, and his administration was attempting to deal with the crisis of the Great Depression. The Roosevelt administration and Congress passed a number of programs—called the New Deal—designed to provide the country with jobs and relief. The legislation gave the federal government wide authority to institute these initiatives.

The nine-member Supreme Court, however, in a series of five-to-four decisions, invalidated much New Deal legislation. The majority argued that Congress had ceded too much legislative power to government agencies.

According to Jeffrey Toobin in a May 24, 2010, article in the *New Yorker*, Roosevelt's response was to propose "a change in the structure of the Court: henceforth, the President would name an additional Justice for each one over the age of seventy. The justification was that the new appointees would assist their elderly colleagues with their work, but, as everyone knew, the real motive was to put enough F.D.R. appointees on the Court to allow the New Deal to proceed."

At first, Roosevelt's plan seemed likely to succeed. In the 1930s, as today, judicial activism tended to be unpopular. When judges overturned the will of elective representatives, the public usually sided overwhelmingly with the elected representatives. In a March 25, 2010, *New York Times* book review of Jeff Shesol's book *Supreme Power: Franklin Roosevelt vs. the Supreme Court*, Alan Brinkley notes, "One of Shesol's many important contributions to an understanding of this controversy is his powerful description of the extraordinary opprobrium the court confronted as it began to overturn New Deal measures in 1935. Indeed, it was the deep unpopularity of the court that helped embolden Roosevelt to challenge it in 1937."

Despite the court's unpopularity, and despite Roosevelt's majorities in Congress, the president's efforts to pack the court with additional justices proved unexpectedly controversial. Republicans, of course, were adamantly opposed to the plan. But even many Democrats opposed it, on the grounds that Roosevelt's actions were, in Brinkley's words, a display of "excessive presidential power and a threat to the Constitution." Opposition to the plan was so great that Roosevelt eventually had to abandon it. The setback "was one of the worst episodes of Roosevelt's presidential career" according to an online article on PBS.org. Roosevelt, the site continued, was "publicly humiliated and utterly defeated." The judicial activists, it seemed, had won.

Victory was not quite so clear-cut, however. Roosevelt had to abandon his plan and suffered political damage as a result. However, "in the end, Roosevelt got what he wanted," according to Christopher Malone in an article in *Law and Politics Book Review*. After Roosevelt applied pressure, some Supreme Court justices began to rule in his favor. Over time others retired and Roosevelt was able to pick their replacements. The court-packing plan died in large part because it became clear to everyone that FDR was going to get his way without it. And sure enough, the Supreme Court began to rule in Roosevelt's favor, declaring New Deal legislation constitutional. Malone concludes that just because the Supreme Court is "the least political branch does not mean that the Supreme Court is wholly divorced from politics." The justices "don't make decisions in a vacuum," Malone concludes, and "the power of judgment will always have political consequences."

The court-packing battle, then, was both a constitutional and a political struggle between the executive and judicial branches. Judicial activism did not prevail, but neither did Roosevelt's executive activism. Instead, the issue was resolved within the institutional framework of the Constitution. As Jeffrey Toobin notes, "Roosevelt lost the court-packing battle, but he won the legal war over the New Deal. By the end of his long tenure in the White House, he had made eight Supreme Court appointments, and that is what guaranteed that the federal government was able to address the economic crisis." Toobin suggests that the best way for presidents to confront judicial activism, therefore, is to win reelection. By doing so, they will gain the opportunity to appoint more justices.

The chapters in this book raise additional questions about judicial activism, including Is Judicial Activism Harmful? How Has Judicial Activism Affected Particular Issues? What Is the Relationship Between Public Opinion and Judicial Activism? and Is Judicial Activism an Issue in Other Countries? The differing viewpoints show that the controversy surrounding judicial activism and the balance between the judicial, executive, and legislative branches continues to be an important issue more than seventy years after FDR's court-packing plan.

OPPOSING
VIEWPOINTS®
SERIES

CHAPTER 1

Is Judicial Activism Harmful?

Chapter Preface

One of the most high-profile and influential opponents of judicial activism is Justice Antonin Scalia of the US Supreme Court. Scalia, who was appointed to the court by Ronald Reagan in 1986, is a strongly conservative justice. He has argued forcefully that judges should abide by the framers' original Constitutional intention. In cases where the Constitution is not clear, he insists, the judiciary should abide by the decision of legislatures.

Thus, for example, in a 2004 speech at Harvard University, Scalia rejected the idea that justices should be arbiters of moral right and wrong. Instead, as reported by Alvin Powell in a September 30, 2004, article in the *Harvard Gazette*, Scalia stated, "What I am questioning is the propriety, indeed the sanity, of having value laden decisions such as these made for the entire society. . . . Nothing I learned from law courses here at Harvard, none of the experiences I acquired in practicing law, qualifies me to decide whether there ought to be a fundamental right to abortion or assisted suicide."

In a January 11, 2011, interview with *California Lawyer*, Scalia further explained that, "In its most important aspects, the Constitution tells the current society that it cannot do [whatever] it wants to do. It is a decision that the society has made that in order to take certain actions, you need the extraordinary effort that it takes to amend the Constitution."

In the same interview, Scalia went on to argue that the Fourteenth Amendment did not initially ban discrimination on the basis of gender, and that, therefore, reading such a ban into the amendment is incorrect. He argues that society can decide that it is wrong to discriminate against women, but that such a guarantee is not in the Constitution itself. Sex discrimination should therefore be prevented by the legislature, Scalia argues, not by the courts.

Though Scalia has taken a vocal stand against judicial activism, he has occasionally been accused of judicial activism himself. Cathy Young in an October 2005 article in *Reason* argues that Scalia's "moral views have a habit of grafting themselves onto his constitutional philosophy." Young notes that Scalia is a social conservative who in his decisions has opposed the legalization of sodomy (anal sex) and has supported preferential treatment for churches. Young argues that Scalia's arguments stem not just from the Constitution's original intent but also from "his idea of a proper civic order—one in which those who do not adhere to traditional religions are, in an important sense, relegated to second-class status." Adam Cohen, writing in an April 19, 2005, *New York Times* article, adds that, "Justice Scalia likes to boast that he follows his strict-constructionist philosophy wherever it leads, even if it leads to results he disagrees with. But it is uncanny how often it leads him just where he already wanted to go."

The remainder of this chapter discusses what should and what should not be considered judicial activism, and whether judicial activism is helpful, harmful, or irrelevant.

| "You can't replace grandpa's liver with a second heart just because you think livers are passé—unless you intend to kill grandpa."

Liberal Activist Judges Endanger the Constitution

Jonathan Witt

Jonathan Witt is a former English professor and a research fellow at the Acton Institute. In the following viewpoint, he argues that the term "living constitution" is misused by liberal activist judges. A living constitution, he says, is not one that changes radically to meet new circumstances, but is rather one that remains true to its original identity and framework. He insists that the Constitution should only be changed through the original mechanism of constitutional amendment and public input, not through the decisions of individual activist judges.

As you read, consider the following questions:

1. What does the author say Justice Oliver Wendell Holmes enabled in the decision *Buck v. Bell?*

2. According to Witt, what were the American founders gambling on when they gathered to compose and sign the Constitution?

3. Witt argues that activist judges have moved to pop off states' rights and replace them with what?

As Senate hearings [in June 2009] gear up for Supreme Court nominee Sonia Sotomayor, an old question is again current: Is the U.S. Constitution a "living document"?

A Living Constitution

Justice Oliver Wendell Holmes first popularized the idea of the Constitution as a protean organism in a 1920 Supreme Court case, *Missouri v. Holland*. There he argued that judges should have broad interpretative latitude in their efforts to keep the Constitution relevant to an evolving society.

Seven years later, in *Buck v. Bell*, Justice Holmes helped clarify just how much latitude he had in mind when he discovered a constitutional right to forcibly sterilize what would eventually be tens of thousands of Americans—many of them poor blacks deemed unfit to breed.

Despite the sorry pedigree of the living-document trope, many others over the ensuing decades continued defending it, including Supreme Court Justice Thurgood Marshall on the 200th anniversary of the Constitution.

In the 2000 presidential campaign, [Democratic candidate] Al Gore went one better, promising to appoint judges "who understand that our Constitution is a living and breathing document." With the additional adjective Gore managed to transform an appealing talking point into something redolent of a '30s horror movie: "It's breathing! It's *ALIVE!*"

Sadly for judicial conservatives, Gore's fellow travelers retreated from his verbal innovation, and once again we were faced with the old problem: How to respond to appealing talk of *a living constitution*.

> ## The "Teasing Imprecision" of Judicial Activism
>
> Critics of [Living Constitutionalism], point out that it appears to be nothing more than results-oriented judicial decision making. By this method modern-day judges discern what they believe the current mores of society are (or more often, what they think society's mores should be) and then mold or create constitutional doctrine to reach their desired end. Thus, Chief Justice William Rehnquist once remarked that Living Constitutionalism "has about it a teasing imprecision that makes it a coat of many colors."
>
> *Kevin Clarkson,*
> *"Living Constitutionalism, or Judicial Activism?"*
> Anchorage Daily News, *August 20, 2010.*
> *http://community.adn.com.*

I mean, think about it. What's the effective response? "No, it's dead, damn it!"?

If you're a prominent conservative with a weakness for this retort, know that they will find you. They will place you in a national television news studio. They will neglect to powder your possibly balding forehead. Then they will roll the cameras. They will use you as a weapon against the very thing you love.

A Mr. Potato Head Constitution

"It's dead!" is a nonstarter rhetorically. And it's false. In a figurative but important sense, our Constitution is a living document. When the American founders gathered to compose and sign it 222 years ago, they were gambling that the principles of liberty they fought for could be passed on from one generation to the next as a living legacy of freedom. And that hope was not misplaced. If the Constitution were already dead—not just battered and abused—judicial activists wouldn't need to move against it incrementally and with all manner of rhetorical legerdemain. They wouldn't need to go on pretending that they were actually striving to faithfully interpret its meaning.

This brings us to the central irony. The very people most inclined to gush about our "living Constitution" treat it like a Mr. Potato Head:

Ooh, states' rights. Let's pop that off and replace it with a metastasizing Commerce Clause.[1] *Oh, and look here in my pocket. A constitutional right to redefine the age-old institution of marriage. Oh and let's tack this one on, too—a constitutional right to kill a half born baby and throw whatever's left in the garbage. If anyone complains, we'll call it "the constitutional right to privacy."*

It's time to pause and take the living-document metaphor seriously. Living things have an internal logic, have functional constraints. They aren't endlessly malleable. You can't replace grandpa's liver with a second heart just because you think livers are passé—unless you intend to kill grandpa.

Our living constitution has and will continue to evolve, but if it's to remain alive, it must do so according to the internal logic, the functional constraints, woven into it from the beginning—namely, the constitutional amendment process. What our founders intended—and what our president swore to preserve, protect, and defend—is an amendment process that demands input from American voters and their elected representatives. It accommodates the present while respecting the past.

It does not involve activist judges—unaccountable to the American voter—speaking in reverential tones about "a living

1. The Commerce Clause of the Constitution gives the federal government the right to regulate trade with other nations and between states.

Constitution" while slowly dismembering its meaning as part of an elaborate word game. This is deconstruction—nihilism. It's where living documents go to die.

> "When Justice [John] Roberts and his colleagues consider transforming the American political landscape to the great benefit of corporate business entities, they are on very uncertain ground as far as their basic judicial legitimacy is concerned."

Conservative Activist Judges Endanger America

Robert A.G. Monks and Peter L. Murray

Robert A.G. Monks is the founder of Lens Governance Advisors, a law firm that advises on corporate governance in the settlement of shareholder litigation; Peter L. Murray is a Harvard Law School visiting professor. In the following viewpoint, they argue that the conservative majority of the John Roberts–led Supreme Court is engaged in judicial activism on behalf of corporations. They say that, with shaky constitutional foundation, the court as led by Roberts is determined to brush aside all limitations on corporate spending on political campaigns. The authors conclude that the court's judicial activism will corrupt the political system.

As you read, consider the following questions:

1. What principle does *Belotti* stand for, according to Monks and Murray?

2. According to Monks and Murray, what did the court decision hold in *McConnell v. Federal Election Commission?*

3. What does judge-made law lack, according to the authors?

One of the phrases bandied about during the confirmation hearings for Judge Sonia Sotomayor's nomination to the United States Supreme Court [in 2009] is "judicial activism"—a tendency of judges to use the cases they decide to implement their own notions of public policy. Of course, all recent Supreme Court nominees have steadfastly denied any shred of judicial activism and have uniformly maintained that the proper role of a judge, even a Supreme Court justice, is to apply existing law, whether constitutional, statutory or precedent, to the facts of the case before him or her. No one has been more outspoken against the evils of judicial activism than Chief Justice [John] Roberts.

Citizens United

Now it appears that the chief may be undertaking a bit of judicial activism of his own. The case is *Citizens United v. FEC [Federal Election Commission]*. The conservative group that sponsored *Hillary: The Movie* [about Democratic presidential candidate and later secretary of state Hillary Clinton] just before the Democratic primary is seeking to avoid or roll back the 2002 McCain-Feingold campaign finance law that prohibits the use of corporate funds to influence elections. Chief Justice Roberts and his conservative Supreme Court majority are getting ready to use *Citizens United* as the vehicle to overrule established precedent (and overturn carefully drafted legislation) and grant business corporations a constitutional right to use their funds to participate in political debate, not only on public issues, but even in the election of candidates to office. Such a move would be judicial activism on a grand scale!

Business corporations and their owners have participated in political life in many ways for many years. Corporate lobbying, campaign contributions by business leaders, "soft money campaign support" by businesses, the "revolving door" of businessmen and public servants: These are only a few of the many ways that corporations interact with politicians and political institutions in an effort to influence public action to their advantage. The American public has learned to live with a strong connection between business and politics.

What is relatively new, however, is the claim that business entities have a *constitutional right* to utilize their economic power to participate in political campaigns and influence the outcome of public votes free of meaningful public regulation. The idea can be traced to the 1978 case of *First National Bank of Boston v. Bellotti*, 435 U.S. 765, where a 5 to 4 majority of the Court voided a Massachusetts law that prohibited corporations from expending funds in connection with state referenda having nothing to do with their business on the ground it was an unconstitutional interference with corporate freedom of speech. In brief, *Bellotti* stands for the principle that corporations may spend money to influence the outcome of a public referendum regardless of whether the issue relates to the corporation's business interests.

Corporate Activism

Bellotti is the handiwork of [Justice] Lewis Powell, the consummate corporate lawyer from Richmond, Virginia, who was drafted to the Supreme Court by Richard Nixon in 1971. Although Powell was considered a moderate on most issues during his fifteen years on the Court, he was an activist to the core in matters affecting corporations and their role in American political life. In fact, only two months before he was nominated, the future justice wrote a secret memorandum to the director of the U.S. Chamber of Commerce on the vital need of corporate America to take a more direct and powerful role in American politics:

> But one should not postpone more direct political action, while awaiting the gradual change in public opinion to be effected through education and information. Business must learn the lesson, long ago learned by labor and other self-interest groups. This is the lesson that political power is necessary; that such power must be assiduously (sic) cultivated; and that when necessary, it must be used aggressively and with determination—without embarrassment and without the reluctance which has been so characteristic of American business.

It is thus not too surprising that it was Powell who wrote the Court's opinion sustaining the First National Bank of Boston's constitutional challenge to the Massachusetts statute.

In holding that the First Amendment of the United States Constitution prevents the states from seriously restricting corporations from using their funds to influence the outcomes of political referenda, Powell reached back to a statement reported to have been made by Chief Justice [Morrison] Waite at the outset of oral argument in a 19th-century railroad tax assessment case, *Santa Clara County v. Southern Pacific R. Co.*, (1886): "The court does not wish to hear argument on the question whether the provision in the Fourteenth Amendment to the Constitution, which forbids a State to deny to any person within its jurisdiction the equal protection of the laws, applies to these corporations. We are all of opinion that it does."

This dictum was in dissonance with the general view that corporations, as artificial creations of the laws of men, enjoyed no "inalienable rights" but only those legal properties that the legislature chooses to give them. While there are numerous cases applying the Due Process Clause of the Fourteenth Amendment to the property of corporations, no case prior to *Bellotti* had suggested that corporations had the rights to freedom of speech, assembly, petition, etc., spelled out in the First Amendment.

Justice Powell's discovery (or invention) of First Amendment rights for corporations in *Bellotti* let a genie out of the bottle. Justice [William] Rehnquist, who dissented in *Bellotti*, recognized that:

> A State grants to a business corporation the blessings of potentially perpetual life and limited liability to enhance its efficiency as an economic entity. It might reasonably be concluded that those properties, so beneficial in the economic sphere, pose special dangers in the political sphere.

Even the *Bellotti* majority acknowledged that allowing corporations to deploy their financial power in elective politics would go too far. In a footnote to the majority opinion, Justice Powell noted that the Massachusetts statute under review also prohibited corporate contributions to candidates or political parties. That portion of the statute was not being challenged and Justice Powell noted how important it was for the government to be able to prevent the corruption of elected officials by contributors. This footnote left open (perhaps even embraced) the idea that Congress still has the power to curb a corporation's use of its economic power to influence candidate elections.

Money and Elections

History since *Bellotti* has affirmed Justice Rehnquist's foresight. The role of money in politics at all levels has burgeoned. Both states and the federal government have been scrambling to get things under some control. At the state level this struggle has brought forth various forms of campaign finance legislation.

A Michigan law that restricted a corporation's ability to use general corporate funds to influence elections of candidates came before the Rehnquist Court In 1990. In *Austin v. Michigan Chamber of Commerce*, (1990), a majority of the Court (including Chief Justice Rehnquist) somewhat narrowed the negative implications of *Bellotti* by ruling that the state *could* prohibit a corporation from spending its own funds in support of a candidate. At the federal level the battle to curb excesses of corporate (and individual) campaign and election spending ultimately resulted in the Bipartisan Campaign Reform Act of 2002, commonly known as "McCain-Feingold" after its Senate sponsors [John McCain and Russ Feingold]. When Congress crafted the prohibitions of corporate electioneering and related political activity in McCain-Feingold it paid careful attention to *Austin* and to footnote 26 in *Bellotti*. The reform legislation contained an express prohibition on corporate funding of "electioneering communications" that referred to a political candidate within 30 days of a primary and 60 days of a general election.

McCain-Feingold was immediately tested by a constitutional challenge in a suit by U.S. Senator Mitch McConnell that reached the Supreme Court in 2003 [*McConnell v. Federal Election Commission*].... McCain-Feingold survived the challenge; the Court's decision held that corporate political speech in the form of "issue advertisements" that are the "functional equivalent" of "electioneering communications" can be legally banned without infringing any corporate constitutional rights of freedom of speech.

Chief Justice John Roberts

Enter Chief Justice John G. Roberts, who was confirmed in 2005. During his hearings the new chief justice repeatedly referred to the role of a Supreme Court justice as akin to that of "umpire." It now appears that the umpire may be about to change the rules of the game.

In *FEC [Federal Election Commission] v. Wisconsin Right to Life*, (2007), the Wisconsin Right to Life [WRL] (a nonprofit corporation subject to the limitations of McCain-Feingold) ran ads encouraging viewers to contact Wisconsin's U.S. senators and urge them to oppose filibusters of Bush administration judicial nominees. The Federal Election Commission deemed the ads to be the "functional equivalent" of electioneering communications and refused to allow them to be aired within 60 days of the election.

The conservative majority of the Roberts Court ruled that the "functional equivalent" test must be applied narrowly, too narrowly to cover the activities of WRL. According to Chief Justice Roberts and his conservative colleagues, unless an ad was reasonably interpreted as urging the support or defeat of a candidate, it was eligible for an "as applied" exception to the McCain-Feingold limits on issue ads close to an election. By construing the statute narrowly, the Court did not have to attack the preexisting authority of *McConnell* or *Austin*, although Justices [Antonin] Scalia, [Clarence] Thomas and [Anthony] Kennedy were ready and eager to do so. As Chief Justice Roberts observed,

> *McConnell* held that express advocacy of a candidate or his opponent by a corporation shortly before an election may be prohibited, along with the functional equivalent of such express advocacy. We have no occasion to revisit that determination today.

The clear implication is that on some "tomorrow" the Court may indeed be ready to overrule *McConnell* and *Austin*. Such a move would unshackle the genie that was first uncorked by Justice Powell in *Bellotti*, and let corporate financial power loose on the election process.

Citizens United may be the case that the Roberts majority has been waiting for. Since it is hard to imagine that a film about then presidential candidate Hillary Clinton can "reasonably be interpreted as anything other than an ad urging the support or defeat of a candidate," Citizens United is asking the Roberts Supreme Court to overrule *McConnell* and kill the "functional equivalent" rule that the Rehnquist Supreme Court crafted only 6 years ago.

The case was argued on March 23, 2009. During the argument it became apparent that some Supreme Court justices may be thinking about the *Citizens United* case as an opportunity to strip away any meaningful restrictions on the ability of corporate America to participate in all aspects of the political process including the election of candidates for public office.

This concern became more concrete when Chief Justice Roberts took the unusual step of setting the case for reargument on September 9. The order for reargument specifically invites the parties to address the issue of whether the *McConnell* or *Austin* precedents should be overruled, either in whole or in part. Enter judicial activism—of the conservative variety.

McConnell and *Austin* are four-square precedents of the United States Supreme Court that establish limits to the corporate free speech genie conjured up in *Bellotti*. Important national legislation is grounded on these precedents. There is no national hue and cry for the repeal of McCain-Feingold or for overruling the judicial foundation of its constitutionality. Certainly there is no indication that *Austin*, *McConnell* or McCain-Feingold have become obsolete or outdated. In fact, all indications are to the contrary. With each successive election the role of corporations and their money is becoming ever more evident.

Austin, *McConnell* and McCain-Feingold sought to place limits on the corporate genie's capacity to do serious mischief on our political institutions. There is good reason now to fear that the Roberts majority may be poised to wipe away these limits in an act of judicial activism that is breathtaking in its implications. Based on the shaky constitutional bases of *Bellotti*, such a decision by the Roberts majority would transform the core of our nation's political structure.

Corporations Are Not Humans

In the context of election to public office, the distinction between corporate and human speakers is significant. Although they make enormous contributions to our society, corporations are not actually members of it. They cannot vote or run for office. Because they may be managed and controlled by nonresidents, their interests may conflict in fundamental respects with the interests of eligible voters. The financial resources, legal structure, and instrumental orientation of corporations raise legitimate concerns about their role in the electoral process. Our lawmakers have a compelling constitutional basis, if not also a democratic duty, to take measures designed to guard against the potentially deleterious effects of corporate spending in local and national races.

John Paul Stevens, dissent in
Citizens United v. Federal Election Commission,
January 21, 2010. www.law.cornell.edu.

The Illegitimacy of *Bellotti*

As noted before, the sole authority for the proposition that the free speech rights of the First Amendment benefits and protects corporate entities as well as natural persons is *First National Bank of Boston v. Bellotti*. At the time the Constitution was originally adopted, corporations were very rare and special entities, created by legislative acts for particular described purposes. The word "corporation" appears nowhere in the Constitution or Bill of Rights. It is scarcely conceivable that the drafters of the Constitution had anything resembling corporate entities in mind when they drafted the Bill of Rights.

For nearly a century it was assumed that the Bill of Rights protected persons, not corporations. The Fourteenth Amendment ban on deprivation of property without due process or equal protection of the law has been consistently applied to property of corporations and natural persons alike. However prior to *Bellotti* there was never any hint that the purely personal rights of the First Amendment or the Bill of Rights belong to corporate entities as well as human beings. As Justice Rehnquist noted in his *Bellotti* dissent, "The question presented today, whether business corporations have any constitutionally protected liberty to engage in political activities, has never been squarely addressed by any previous decision of this court."

The lack of legal foundation for *Bellotti* together with its disturbing policy considerations have been pointed out in legal literature ever since the case came down in 1978. That the Court may be on the verge of taking a step for which *Bellotti* is the main basis of support demonstrates the lengths to which the Roberts majority is prepared to go to promote corporate "rights."

Judge-made law does not have the democratic legitimacy of measures that have been adopted by legislatures and ratified by executive action. Judges are not legislators. They are not, and should not be, politically accountable to anyone. They do not take part in the political debate concerning the matters that they decide.

The lack of democratic legitimacy for judges and their rulings counsels a degree of restraint in the creation of judge-made law. Such restraint is even more important when judges are confronted with the potential of transforming by their own decisions the structure or function of essential political institutions.

The common-law system gives courts the authority to develop rules of law based on accretion of case-by-case decisions. Such a system has decided strengths in the creation of responsive doctrines of private law governing the legal dealings of private actors with each other. On the other hand, the authority of public law, particularly laws establishing the structure and function of various participants in the political process, derives entirely from the democratic composition of the law-giving body. Widely representative legislative bodies can act to restructure American politics and can be held accountable for their actions in political elections. On the other hand, when courts act to change the political playing field, they are in no way accountable for the havoc that their decisions may wreak. Ever since the founding of the Republic, the United States Supreme Court has been conscious of this issue and has refrained from adjudicating issues of political structure and role and has deferred to the democratically constituted legislature in these matters.

Thus, when Justice Roberts and his colleagues consider transforming the American political landscape to the great benefit of corporate business entities, they are on very uncertain ground as far as their basic judicial legitimacy is concerned.

Corruption of the Political Process

Now that 30 years have passed since Justice Powell took a prefatory comment in a 19th-century railroad case and used it to enfranchise corporations in the political process, events have shown that it is *Bellotti*, not the cases that tried to limit its mischief, which should be up for reconsideration. The incredible growth of corporate presence in all forms of political activity has indeed brought about the corruption of the political process that Justice Powell acknowledged might occur if corporate enterprises were allowed to employ their resources to influence the election of candidates. The "problem of corruption of elected representatives through the creation of political debts" has become the American political reality in the 21st century. Why not put *Bellotti* on the table for reconsideration when the Court convenes on September 9 [2009]?

Emboldened by *Bellotti*, corporations have indeed taken the program of the Powell memorandum to heart. The number of registered lobbyists in Washington has increased from 3,400 in 1977 to almost 34,000 in 2006. In the 2008 House and Senate races $400 million dollars was raised and spent for candidates by political action committees, mostly linked to business corporations. Corporate spending for such events as the inauguration, party conventions and even presidential debates has become embarrassingly blatant.

A recent study [by the Public Campaign Action Fund] of the relationship of health care industry campaign support to positions of congressmen on health care reform concluded,

> These findings also point to a need to address the fundamental problem in the financing of American politics. Members of Congress spend time courting donors when they could be passing legislation, building relationships with other lawmakers, or addressing constituents' needs. With ever-increasing campaign costs, members follow the infamous bank robber Willie Sutton's advice to go to "where the money is"—the industries regulated by their committees. That only makes the public more skeptical that policy is for sale.

It is now clear that Justice Powell's judicial activism in *Bellotti* has not stood the test of time. The notion that artificial legal entities organized to facilitate the transaction of business and the accumulation of wealth should have constitutionally protected rights that the framers believed came to human beings from their Creator has even less credibility today than in 1978. Certainly the amorality of corporate America has only become clearer since Justice Powell gave corporations political rights. A fair-minded and conservative Court, in tune with traditional values of all Americans, would take the opportunity posed by *Citizens United* to reconsider the juridical basis on which *McConnell* and *Austin* are being attacked rather than consider overruling these useful and important mainstream precedents. It is instead *Bellotti* that should be overruled to give our public institutions a chance to escape the corruption of corporate money that is overwhelming politics at all levels.

The evident intention of the Roberts Court to undermine, roll back and ultimately overrule the useful *McConnell* and *Austin* precedents is the very kind of judicial activism that Chief Justice Roberts and his conservative brethren have so consistently deplored. In fact, the activism that Justice Roberts is now contemplating goes far beyond even such "activist" decisions as *Roe v. Wade*. The conservative activists of the Roberts Court are poised to turn over the American elective process to the tender mercies of Corporate America. Sadly, it appears that our judicial tradition of constitutional restraint with respect to issues affecting politics may be out the window when an opportunity arises to increase the power and influence of America's corporate entities. The many senators who have expressed concern over judicial activism in the Sotomayor hearings need only look to the Roberts Court on September 9 for an example of judicial activism that will take our breath away.

> *"By relying on the opinions of judges instead of principles grounded in the Constitution, [judicial activism] represents a denial of the rule of law that was the very purpose of the Constitution."*

Judicial Activism, by Liberals and Conservatives, Is a Danger to America

Carson Holloway

Carson Holloway is an associate professor of political science at the University of Nebraska at Omaha. In the following viewpoint, he argues that both liberal and conservative judges engage in judicial activism. In fact, he notes that judicial activism has become embedded in judicial practice through such principles as strict scrutiny. This principle holds that some laws must meet a higher test of constitutionality than others. Holloway argues that strict scrutiny is itself not constitutional and that it leads to further encouragement of judicial activism. He concludes that rampant judicial activism requires a reconsideration of the role of the judiciary in American law.

As you read, consider the following questions:

1. What did the Supreme Court decide in *Boumediene v. Bush*, according to Holloway?

2. When does Holloway say that the elements of the strict scrutiny test first began to emerge in the United States?

3. On what grounds does Holloway argue that the court cannot find clear guidance by looking to the values of contemporary society?

The Supreme Court's recent decision [as of February 2010] regarding corporate spending on political advocacy—*Citizens United v. Federal Election Commission*—provoked the widespread renewal of a long-standing liberal complaint: namely, that the conservative critique of judicial activism is mere hypocrisy. In this case, it was suggested, conservative justices, applauded by conservative commentators, struck down a democratically enacted law and overturned long-established judicial precedents. Surely, the argument runs, this is judicial activism, and surely it reveals the critique of judicial activism as just a convenient tool by which conservatives decry decisions to which they object for political reasons, cloaking their real concerns in feigned constitutional principles.

Liberals, Conservatives, and the Constitution

Though common, this charge of hypocrisy sheds little real light on the questions in relation to which it is invoked, for several reasons. First, it does nothing to help us determine the relative merits of the liberal and conservative positions with regard to the proper exercise of the judicial power. After all, the charge clearly cuts both ways. In regard to *Citizens United*, liberals have complained not only about conservative inconsistency on the matter of judicial activism, but also about the supposed activism of the decision itself. Thus conservatives might well ask these liberal critics: Where was *your* hot indignation about judicial activism when the Court, as recently as nineteen months ago, issued its ruling in *Boumediene v. Bush*? In that case, the Court, to widespread liberal acclaim, reinterpreted key precedents and struck down congressional enactments on the basis of a hitherto unknown right of alien enemy combatants to *habeas corpus* review [that is, to a trial to see if the enemy is legally held]. Liberals no less than conservatives, it seems, can be charged with a selective opposition to judicial activism.

Second, charges of inconsistency regarding judicial activism are often unhelpful because they routinely use the term too loosely—that is, without reference to the merits of the specific constitutional arguments in question. When the Court strikes down a law or overturns precedent, those who disagree with the ruling will generally complain of judicial activism. Yet it is agreed on all sides in American politics that it is sometimes perfectly appropriate for the Court to strike down laws or overturn precedents. After all, from the beginning of the American republic it has been understood that the exercise of judicial review is an inescapable part of the Court's function, and judicial review is inseparable from the possibility of declaring unconstitutional laws void and erroneous precedents inoperative. If judicial activism is to have any useful meaning, then, it will have to be understood as the exercise of judicial review in a way that is not warranted by the Constitution. The purpose of judicial review, however, is to safeguard and enforce the law of the Constitution. Judicial activism, therefore, is best understood not as the striking down of laws or reversing of precedents—both of which may be required by the Court's duty in a particular case—but as the substitution of the Court's political, policy, or moral judgments for the requirements of the law and the Constitution. On this understanding, it is worth observing, the Court could engage in ju-

"The Honorable Justice vs. The Judicial Activist" by Jesse Springer. Copyright © 2005 by Cartoonstock Ltd. Reproduced by permission.

dicial activism even when *upholding* a law or precedent, if it does so contrary to the clear meaning of the Constitution.

Strict Scrutiny

This brings us, in the third place, to a deeper problem: Loosely framed charges of judicial activism, flung selectively by both conservatives and liberals, tend to obscure the disturbing extent to which much of the modern Supreme Court's jurisprudence is itself a product of and a continuing invitation to a problematic judicial activism in the precise sense noted above. That is, the intellectual framework that all the justices, left and right, have inherited, and within which they think they must work, arose from and invites the substitution of their moral and political convictions for the law of the Constitution.

This problem is evident in the Court's opinion in the *Citizens United* case, whether or not one agrees with its ruling. In deciding the question before them, the majority had recourse not only to the Constitution, but also to a Court-created judicial doctrine known as "strict scrutiny." Strict scrutiny is ordinarily applied to laws that (among other things) impose on what the Court regards as "fundamental rights"—such as, in *Citizens United*, the freedom of speech. The test reverses the usual presumption of constitutionality. That is, when strict scrutiny is invoked, the burden of proof is not on the litigant challenging the law to demonstrate its unconstitutionality, but on the government to justify its constitutional legitimacy. Despite weighting the scales against such laws, strict scrutiny further stipulates that they can be upheld if they serve a "compelling governmental interest" by the "least restrictive means." In other words, a law may constitutionally intrude on a fundamental right, if it is necessary to serve some important objective and there is no other way to do so that is less of an intrusion.

Strict scrutiny, however, is itself a product of judicial activism understood as the substitution of the opinions of judges for the requirements of the Constitution. As Justice Felix Frankfurter—one of the Supreme Court's great defenders of judicial restraint—pointed out when the elements of the strict scrutiny test first began to emerge in the mid-twentieth century, there is nothing in the Constitution on the basis of which an impartial reader could conclude that some kinds of laws are entitled to a presumption of constitutionality while others are not. There is, in fact, nothing in the Constitution to suggest that some governmental objectives are more "compelling" than others, or that some rights are more "fundamental" than others. Such categories were utterly unheard of in American constitutional jurisprudence during the nation's first century and a half. They were unknown to Chief Justice [John] Marshall, and even to zealous judicial defenders of rights in the early decades following the ratification of the Fourteenth Amendment. These concepts are not requirements of the Constitution but the inventions of judges seeking to guide the Court to outcomes they approved on nonconstitutional grounds—namely, their own assessment of what would be good and just.

A product of judicial activism, strict scrutiny is also an invitation to ongoing judicial activism. Most obviously, its abandonment of the traditional presumption of constitutionality gives the Court much greater freedom to strike down laws that have been approved by majorities of the people's representatives. Perhaps more important, by requiring the Court to ask questions to which the Constitution provides no answers, strict scrutiny calls judges to substitute their own convictions for those of legislators. What counts as a compelling governmental interest? The Constitution, again, is silent on this question. The answer is not a matter of constitutional law but of political philosophy. Some people think that the promotion of greater economic equality is a compelling governmental interest, while others do not. Some people think that the fostering of traditional sexual morality is a compelling governmental interest, which others would deny. Such disputes are subject to more or less plausible philosophic reasoning, but not to constitutionally conclusive reasoning. When a Court overturns a law based on arguments that are not constitutionally compelling, however, it has not vindicated the Constitution but simply decided to prefer what seems reasonable to it over what seemed reasonable to legislators. It has, in other words, engaged in judicial activism.

Reconsider the Role of the Court

Nor is it the case, as some might contend, that the Court could find clear guidance on what constitutes a compelling governmental interest by looking not to its members' convictions but to the dominant practices and values of contemporary society. The very fact that cases arise in which the parties contend over what is a compelling governmental interest shows that society is characterized as much by division as by agreement on such questions. And when the Court decides to side with one understanding over another without a constitutional reason to do so, it has again engaged in what can plausibly be called judicial activism.

None of this is necessarily to say that the Supreme Court erred in its decision in *Citizens United*. The case involved a law that regulated political speech. Accordingly, even dispensing with strict scrutiny, a Court could reasonably conclude that while such a law is entitled, like any other, to a presumption of constitutionality, that presumption is here overcome by the law's infringement on a freedom expressly enshrined in the text of the Constitution. My point is that, even if *Citizens United* was correctly decided, the use of tests like strict scrutiny, now deeply entrenched in the Court's jurisprudence, drive the Court into kinds of inquiries that almost inevitably make even the most sincere critics of judicial activism engage in it themselves.

Judicial activism is a problem of profound significance for the American republic. By relying on the opinions of judges instead of principles grounded in the Constitution, it represents a denial of the rule of law that was the very purpose of the Constitution. More than that, because the concepts essential to modern judicial activism are so pliable, and because the composition of the Court changes so regularly, judicial activism turns out to be incompatible with the rule of law in any sense. The Court's jurisprudence becomes instead a record of *ad hoc* approvals and disapprovals on the basis of which no clear predictions of future rulings are possible, a set of arbitrary judgments that is the opposite of the rule of law. If this very real and serious problem is to be addressed, our concerns about judicial activism will have to become more than just rhetorical weapons wielded when politically convenient. We will instead have to reconsider the role the Court has assumed for itself over the last half century or more.

"The courts have been at their historic best when rejecting the will of the majority and acting in defense of individual rights."

Judicial Activism in Support of Individual Liberty Is Beneficial

Damon W. Root

Damon W. Root is an associate editor of Reason *magazine and* Reason.com. *In the following viewpoint, he argues that judicial restraint means allowing a majority to decide on legal matters. Root notes that this can often result in an infringement of minority rights. He concludes that the proper role for courts is to engage in limited judicial activism, in which justices intervene to protect individual liberties.*

As you read, consider the following questions:

1. According to Justice Antonin Scalia, what should the courts do when the Constitution is vague or unclear?

2. What did James Madison say the judiciary should act as?

Damon W. Root, "In Defense of Judicial Activism," Reason.com, September 23, 2008. Copyright ©2008 by Reason Foundation. Reproduced by permission.

3. According to the author, what was at issue in the case *Pierce v. Society of Sisters*?

Since joining the United States Supreme Court in 1986, Associate Justice Antonin Scalia has emerged as perhaps America's foremost champion of judicial restraint, the idea that judges should defer to the will of legislative majorities, striking down only those laws that unequivocally run afoul of specifically enumerated constitutional rights. For instance, in his dissent in *Lawrence v. Texas* (2003), where the majority nullified a state law banning homosexual activity, Scalia argued that the Texas legislature's "hand should not be stayed through the invention of a brand-new 'constitutional right' by a Court that is impatient of democratic change." Indeed, "it is the premise of our system that those judgments are to be made by the people, and not imposed by a governing caste that knows best."

Justice Scalia and Judicial Activism

Look up Scalia's dissents in cases as different as *Planned Parenthood v. Casey* (1992), where the majority upheld abortion rights, or *Boumediene v. Bush* (2008), where the Court recognized habeas corpus rights for enemy combatants, and you'll find similar arguments. As Scalia likes to say, when the Constitution is vague or unclear, the courts should let the people, via their elected representatives, have their way.

So it's no small matter that one of the country's most prominent conservative judges is now criticizing Scalia for being a judicial activist. In a provocative new article forthcoming from the *Virginia Law Review*, federal appeals court judge J. Harvie Wilkinson III surveys Scalia's recent handiwork in the landmark gun rights case *D.C. [District of Columbia] v. Heller*[1] (2008) and finds it seriously lacking. "*Heller*," Wilkinson writes,

1. In *District of Columbia v. Heller*, the Supreme Court overturned a handgun ban in Washington, D.C.

"encourages Americans to do what conservative jurists warned for years they should not do: bypass the ballot and seek to press their political agenda in the courts."

In fact, Wilkinson compares Scalia's opinion in *Heller* to the Court's recognition of abortion rights in *Roe v. Wade* (1973), which is about the worst thing one judicial conservative could say to another. In Wilkinson's view, *Heller* grounded a debatable right in an ambiguous piece of constitutional text, it opened the door to decades of future litigation, it disregarded clear legislative preferences, and it aggrandized the judiciary at the expense of the other branches and the people—"the same sins," he argues, that made *Roe* so odious.

Wilkinson certainly has a point. Following Scalia's own rhetoric of modesty and restraint, why should the Supreme Court substitute its wisdom for that of the local officials directly accountable to the inhabitants of Washington, D.C.? What makes handgun bans and mandatory trigger locks clearly unconstitutional but not other "long-standing prohibitions," to borrow Scalia's phrase? More importantly, why entangle the federal courts in the political thicket at all? As Justice John Paul Stevens noted in his dissent, "no one has suggested that the political process is not working exactly as it should in mediating the debate between advocates and opponents of gun control."

Judicial Restraint Means Majority Rule

That's the key point (though Scalia is typically the justice making it). With rare exception, judicial restraint means letting the majority rule. Wilkinson, who clearly disapproves of D.C.'s gun ban, is at least consistent about it. But the whole point of the judiciary is to actively police the other branches, to act, as James Madison put it, as "an impenetrable bulwark against every assumption of power in the legislative or executive."

Wilkinson gets that exactly backwards, writing, "The largest threat to liberty still lies in handing our democratic destiny to the courts." But in fact, the courts have been at their historic best when rejecting the will of the majority and acting in defense of individual rights.

Take *Pierce v. Society of Sisters* (1925). At issue was an Oregon initiative, which had been spearheaded by the Ku Klux Klan and other anti-Catholic groups, requiring that all children between the ages of eight and 16 attend public school. In his opinion for the unanimous Court, Justice James McReynolds declared that, "the child is not the mere creature of the state" and nullified Oregon's law for unreasonably interfering "with the liberty of parents and guardians to direct the upbringing and education of children under their control."

Under Wilkinson's vision of judicial restraint, however, the Court somehow got it wrong in *Pierce* yet got it right in *Korematsu v. United States* (1944), where it deferred to President Franklin Roosevelt, upholding his wartime internment of Japanese Americans. In both cases, Wilkinson's argument is that if the voters have a problem, they should turn to the ballot box, not the courts.

If anything, such examples confirm that the last thing we need is more or better judicial restraint. What we need is a principled form of judicial activism, one that consistently upholds individual liberty while strictly limiting state power. Too bad neither the right nor the left seem very interested in that.

| "Maybe the opposite of an activist court is a court too passive to do justice at all."

Judicial Activism in Support of Justice Is Beneficial

Dahlia Lithwick

Dahlia Lithwick is a contributing editor at Newsweek *and a senior editor at* Slate. *In the following viewpoint, she argues that, while judicial activism has dangers, so do demands for judicial restraint. She says that the courts were established to prevent injustice and discrimination against the powerless. When courts refuse to act, she argues, powerful corporations and interests can trample on individual rights. She concludes that the inactivity of the Supreme Court under Chief Justice John Roberts has made it harder for individuals to find justice in the courts.*

As you read, consider the following questions:

1. What does Lithwick say that we've learned is the opposite of an activist judge?

2. According to Jeffrey Toobin, with whom has Chief Justice Roberts sided during his time on the court?

3. What did Barack Obama say he was looking for in a Supreme Court replacement for John Paul Stevens, according to Lithwick?

Last Friday [in April 2010], Justice Antonin Scalia delivered the Henry J. Abraham lecture at the University of Virginia law school. In defending his constitutional methodology of originalism, Justice Scalia started with a classic joke. I'll paraphrase: Two hunters find themselves being chased through the woods by a bloodthirsty bear. The heavier one starts to huff and puff, and finally turns to the other and wheezes: "I don't think we're going to be able to outrun him!" The second hunter, jogging just ahead, replies: "I don't need to outrun *him*; I only need to outrun *you*!"

The Hazards of Originalism

Scalia's point is that it's not his responsibility to prove that textualism or originalism are perfect constitutional theories. It's enough for him to demonstrate they are better than the alternative. And the alternative, says Scalia, is for a justice to "make the law what he thinks it should be." His parable of the Bear, the Hunters, and the Originalist reminded me of what Scalia does so well that liberal constitutional thinkers can't always manage. Where he is pithy and clear in his prescription for judicial restraint, they get all tangled up in an effort to make their own jurisprudential theory sound perfect. Perhaps in advance of what is shaping up to be a galactic fight about President [Barack] Obama's next Supreme Court nominee, liberals should take Scalia's adage to heart and content themselves just to outrun the other guy. In other words, maybe there is no time like the present to tell the country about the hazards and pitfalls of the conservative theories of originalism and textualism and the cult of balls-and-strikes-ism that has taken over the American jurisprudential debate.

The public conversation about the judiciary in recent decades has often conflated a broad fear of unelected judges with a clear definition of what judges *should* do. In the wake of the Jackson Pollock–style jurisprudence of the Warren court [led by Chief Justice Earl Warren, 1953–1969], anxiety about overreaching judges morphed into a widespread sense that judges simply do too much. Conservative groups happily pushed the line that liberal judges were all merely unelected "activists" bent on "legislating from the bench." But this says little about how a judge should decide cases and much about our fear of the bench. Originalism and textualism aren't the only way to constrain judges, but they dovetail nicely with the idea that if you confine yourself to what the framers would want, you can't make as much of a mess with the yellow paint.

That's how judicial "activism"—a word we all should acknowledge is meaningless—turned into a catchall term for judges who did anything one didn't like. They were, after all, acting. It's only in recent years that we've discovered that the opposite of an "activist" judge is, in fact, a deceased one.

Siding with the Powerful

When John Roberts captured the hearts of America during his confirmation hearing, with his language of "minimalism" and "humility" and "restraint," he brilliantly reassured Americans that at his very best, he would do just about nothing from the bench. This pledge was shored up by a complex web of doctrines guaranteed to ensure that, in case after case, his hands were tied. Long before he was tapped for a seat at the high court, Roberts had written approvingly of efforts to cabin judicial power, including his efforts in 1984 to promote court-stripping legislation, to circumscribe the reach of Title IX, and to stiffen standing requirements for access to courts. Since becoming chief justice, Roberts and his colleagues on the court's right wing have continued to resolve cases by narrowing the authority of courts to solve problems. The Roberts court has worked to ensure that it's harder for women to bring gender-discrimination suits and harder for elderly Americans to sue

Roberts Is More than Just an Umpire

When Antonin Scalia joined the Court, in 1986, he brought a new gladiatorial spirit to oral arguments, and in subsequent years the justices have often used their questions as much for campaign speeches as for requests for information. Roberts, though, has taken this practice to an extreme, and now, even more than the effervescent Scalia, it is the chief justice, with his slight Midwestern twang, who dominates the Court's public sessions.

Roberts's hard-edged performance at oral argument offers more than just a rhetorical contrast to the rendering of himself that he presented at his confirmation hearing. "Judges are like umpires," Roberts said at the time. "Umpires don't make the rules. They apply them. The role of an umpire and a judge is critical. They make sure everybody plays by the rules. But it is a limited role. Nobody ever went to a ball game to see the umpire." His jurisprudence as chief justice, Roberts said, would be characterized by "modesty and humility." After four years on the Court, however, Roberts's record is not that of a humble moderate but, rather, that of a doctrinaire conservative.

Jeffrey Toobin, "No More Mr. Nice Guy,"
New Yorker, *May 25, 2009. www.newyorker.com.*

for age discrimination. It's ever harder for those affected by pollution to prevail. Last term [2008–2009] was the worst ever for environmental cases at the high court.

Reviewing these trends at the Roberts court last spring, Jeffrey Toobin concluded that

> [t]he kind of humility that Roberts favors reflects a view that the Court should almost always defer to the existing

power relationships in society. In every major case since he became the nation's seventeenth chief justice, Roberts has sided with the prosecution over the defendant, the state over the condemned, the executive branch over the legislative, and the corporate defendant over the individual plaintiff.

You can keep on characterizing this as merely "calling balls and strikes," but it's becoming amply clear to most Americans that with this court behind the plate, only big business ever gets to first.

We have, then, a surrendered court, an institution devoted to the principle that it is critically important to be seen as powerless and unimportant. A court that has deployed filing deadlines and pleading requirements and standing doctrine to keep the courts out of the picture. Maybe it's not as simple as "restraint" versus "activism." Maybe the opposite of an activist court is a court too passive to do justice at all.

Now before my friends out there in the conservative blogosphere go crazy and consign me to the same place they consign, well, everyone I know, it's important to clarify that there is a principled jurisprudential debate to be had, on the need to constrain the judiciary. There is a need for a thoughtful discussion about how to interpret the Constitution and what judges should take into consideration while doing so, and I dearly hope we will spend the coming weeks having it. My only point here is that most Americans, having been terrified by the specter of "liberal activist" judges legislating from the bench, should be equally terrified at the prospect of "humble judicial minimalists" who are institutionally powerless to do anything at all to protect America's women, its workers, its minorities, and its environment. I suspect most Americans still want to believe that if they are the victims of discrimination or injustice or brutality, the courts are a place to go for vindication. As suspicious as we may all have become of ideological, activist judges, I imagine most of us would still like to believe that if we were to file something in a courthouse tomorrow, a judge would be available to do something about it.

A Positive Case for Activity

If I learned anything from the confirmation hearing last week [in April 2010] for Goodwin Liu, Obama's nominee for the U.S. Court of Appeals for the 9th Circuit, it's that the Republican script about judges won't change anytime soon. Anyone nominated by a Democrat will be reflexively accused of being dangerous, grandiose, power-mad, and unprincipled. It's worked for years, and it may even work for a few more months. But faced with a federal judiciary proving itself to be so "humble" and "restrained" that it should maybe be on Philip Morris' payroll, the idea that there is an affirmative role for jurists to play in this system of checks and balances should not be so hard to sell.

In his excellent piece in the *New York Times* last week, professor Geoffrey R. Stone talked about the need to do away with conclusory language about neutral umpires versus judges who make stuff up. Invoking the vital constitutional role of the court in protecting minorities, Stone pointed out that the court cannot play its role as a counter-majoritarian check when conservative judges "tend to exercise the power of judicial review to invalidate laws that disadvantage corporations, business interests, the wealthy and other powerful interests in society." Again, there is a compelling argument to be made to the contrary. But Stone's larger point is that we can't have this conversation when we are busy bonking one another on the head with bats that say "crazy activist" and "neutral umpire."

Writing yesterday at the *Huffington Post*, Simon Lazarus also observed that while "in the recent past, Democratic leaders have shrunk from controversies about the Constitution and the courts" this nomination seems to have motivated the White House and congressional Democrats to refine their

message to something beyond "We. Are. So *Not*. Activists."
What we have heard, since the day of [Justice John Paul]
Stevens' retirement, has been a sharp response from President
Obama himself, who said he was looking for a justice who,
like retiring Justice John Paul Stevens, "knows that in a democracy, powerful interests must not be allowed to drown out
the voices of ordinary citizens." Sen. Patrick Leahy has made
the same point in the weeks since, insisting on the Sunday
talk shows that under the guise of in-activism, the Roberts
court has almost completely ceded its responsibility to see justice done in America. Props to both the White House and
Sen. Leahy, who seem to have taken Justice Scalia's lesson to
heart: This time around, liberals needn't try to outrun the
bear. They just have to outrun a Roberts court that is increasingly reluctant to move.

> *"The choice is not between activists and umpires; it is between different ideological approaches to judging."*

Judicial Activism Is Not a Useful Concept

Kermit Roosevelt

Kermit Roosevelt is a professor at the University of Pennsylvania Law School and author of The Myth of Judicial Activism. *In the following viewpoint, he argues that the law does not provide clear, objective answers to many constitutional questions. As a result, he says, judges have latitude to make different decisions on a single issue without being activists. He says that the real difference between conservative and liberal judges is not activism but empathy for the powerless. He says conservatives tend to decide in favor of the powerful while liberals decide in favor of those with less political power.*

As you read, consider the following questions:

1. What do Orrin Hatch and Karl Rove say that empathy is a code word for, according to Roosevelt?

2. President Obama says that empathy is the quality of what?

3. Why does the author say all responsible people should oppose the use of the word "activism"?

Empathy, the *Oxford English Dictionary* tells us, is "the power of projecting one's personality into (and so fully comprehending) the object of contemplation." Recently, in response to President [Barack] Obama's announcement that it was a quality he would seek in Supreme Court nominees, Orrin Hatch and Karl Rove have offered a different definition. Empathy, they say, is a "code word" for liberal judicial activism.

The Law Does Not Provide Clear Answers

That definition might be useful to the debate over judicial qualifications if activism were itself a helpful concept. But it is not.

Activism, in political rhetoric, means deciding cases based on a judge's policy preferences rather than the law. That is certainly a bad thing, but it is almost never possible to say with confidence that the Supreme Court has engaged in it. The constitutional provisions that generate controversial cases tend to indicate that some value is important—equality, for instance, or free speech—but they do not mark the outer boundaries of the concept or tell the Court how to apply it in particular circumstances. "The law" does not provide a clear answer in these hard cases, and since it doesn't, one cannot say that judges have rejected law in favor of policy.

So how does the Court decide a hard constitutional case? The most basic choice it has to make is how assertive it will be with respect to the other branches of government. Will it defer to their judgment? Or will it press its own vision of equality or free speech against the contrary view of Congress or a state?

Liberal and conservative judges tend to show different patterns of assertiveness and deference. Explaining his vote against the nomination of John Roberts, the then senator Obama noted that Roberts "has far more often used his formidable skills on behalf of the strong in opposition to the weak." If there is a theme emerging from the decisions of the Roberts Court, it is precisely that. The Roberts Court tends to be assertive in defending the interests of the powerful. It intervened in the name of equality when whites were inconvenienced by an attempt to maintain an integrated school system. It protected the speech of corporations hoping to influence elections, but not that of a public school student and a government employee facing discipline for their words.

Liberal judges, by contrast, tend to assert their authority on behalf of the politically weak. With respect to free speech, the Court's liberals voted in favor of the suspended student and the fired employee and against the corporations. On equality, they would have left the integration plan up to the political process. Liberal interventions in the name of equality tend to come on behalf of minorities.

Not Activism, but Empathy

What explains the difference between the liberals and conservatives? The dichotomy between law and policy is no help here. Neither is the idea of activism, or facile analogies about judges being umpires rather than players. But empathy, as Obama described it, actually does a pretty good job.

Empathy, he said, is the quality of "understanding and identifying with people's hopes and struggles." A judge with this quality will be more ready to believe that the political process fails to protect the rights of the weak and the unpopular. She will be more sensitive to the plight of the outsider and more willing to see fundamental similarities between people, rather than believe that others are irreconcilably different. (That is the central issue in the current struggle over gay rights, as it was in the civil rights movement of the last century.) She will be less willing to suppose that the unfortunate necessarily deserve their fate.

A judge who held these views (I do not mean to suggest that [Sonia] Sotomayor [an Obama appointee, later confirmed to the Supreme Court] does or does not) would tend to assert judicial power on behalf of political outsiders rather than corporate interests or majority groups. She would believe that the political process could generally be trusted to safeguard the rights of the powerful, but she would be more suspicious of political outcomes that disfavored the weak. As far as current political alignments go, she would be liberal. She would not, however, be activist in any useful sense of the word. And her critics would not be neutral defenders of the Constitution but rather purveyors of a particular, conservative ideology.

That ideological stance is what talk of activism seeks to camouflage. No one thinks that judges should decide cases based on policy rather than law, and if a nominee is truly an activist, all responsible people should oppose her. But the choice is not between activists and umpires; it is between different ideological approaches to judging. What all responsible people should oppose is the misleading word "activism." We cannot have a meaningful discussion about the courts or the Constitution in those terms.

It is to Obama's credit that when he was a senator opposing a nominee, he did not resort to vapid slogans. He admitted that in some cases, law alone would not provide answers. And he said forthrightly that he feared in such cases Roberts would side with the strong, as indeed he has. The conservative critics of empathy are entitled to their views, but they must likewise make their case on the merits. And they should be prepared to hear in response that on ideological issues, elections have consequences.

Periodical and Internet Sources Bibliography

The following articles have been selected to supplement the diverse views presented in this chapter.

Robert Barnes	"Recent High Court Cases Revive Debate on Judicial Activism," *Washington Post*, May 3, 2010.
Clint Bolick	"A Cheer for Judicial Activism," *Wall Street Journal*, April 3, 2007.
Adam Cohen	"Are Liberal Judges Really 'Judicial Activists,'" *Time*, June 9, 2010.
Marcia Coyle	"Is Sotomayor a Judicial Activist? New Studies May Shed Some Light," *National Law Journal*, June 8, 2009.
E.J. Dionne	"Ceding the Court," *New Republic*, July 5, 2010.
Richard Garnett	"*Citizens United* and 'Conservative Judicial Activism,'" *National Review Online*, January 21, 2010. www.nationalreview.com.
Ben Johnson	"Sotomayor's Racialist Judicial Activism," *FrontPage Magazine*, June 26, 2009. http://archive.frontpagemag.com.
Jack Kenny	"Souter's Defense of Judicial Activism," *New American*, May 29, 2010.
Ramesh Ponnuru	"When Judicial Activism Suits the Right," *New York Times*, June 23, 2009.
Jeffrey Toobin	"Activism vs. Restraint," *New Yorker*, May 24, 2010.
David L. Tubbs	"Revisiting Judicial Review," *American Spectator*, October 2009.

How Has Judicial Activism Affected Particular Issues?

Chapter Preface

In 2010 Congress passed a sweeping health care overhaul called the Patient Protection and Affordable Care Act (PPACA). The reform was a central legislative goal of President Barack Obama, who signed the bill into law on March 23.

Health care reform was controversial. The US health care system was widely regarded as expensive and poorly designed; many people could not obtain insurance, and health care costs were much higher than in other Western countries. On the other hand, many conservatives and Republicans argued that the reform gave the government too much control over the health care system. In particular, conservatives were angered by health care mandates—provisions in the bill that made it a legal requirement for everyone in the United States to purchase health insurance.

Many commentators argued that the mandates were unconstitutional. Specifically, they claimed that the mandates violated the commerce clause of the Constitution, which states that the federal government has the power "[t]o regulate commerce with foreign nations, and among the several States, and with the Indian Tribes." Those who supported a strict reading of the commerce clause argued that the federal government's authority should be limited to trade. The government should not be allowed to force individuals to purchase health insurance.

Thus, John Yoo in a December 13, 2010, article on Ricochet.com argued that, "The Commerce Clause, as originally understood, would not have covered individual health care decisions. But it has been read to allow the government to prohibit the individual from making, buying, or selling products, of even the smallest amount, because they are part of an interstate market in the good." William J. Watkins writing in a

December 21, 2010, article in the *Christian Science Monitor* added, "Divorced from historical meanings and the original intent of the framers, the Commerce Clause has become the fount of unlimited government. Obamacare is but the latest episode of rampant commerce abuse. If the individual insurance mandate passes constitutional muster and enters the realm of precedent, then we can safely assume that no right, liberty, or inactivity is protected from the schemes of Washington's lawgivers."

Watkins and Yoo believe that judges need to strike down the individual mandate in order to protect the Constitution and prevent the spread of federal power. Others, however, have argued that court action to undermine health care reform would be an example of judicial activism. University of Pennsylvania professor Jeff Weintraub in an April 3, 2010, post on his blog, noted that the commerce clause has often been interpreted broadly—as early as 1798, in fact, the government actually required sailors to purchase health insurance. Weintraub concluded that the law should not be discarded, but suggested that the "exceptionally and aggressively activist Supreme Court" led by Chief Justice John Roberts might repeal it anyway. Weintraub added that "we are living through an era of exceptionally unabashed judicial activism," in which conservative justices disregard congressional decisions in order to impose their own view of the law.

As of January 2011, federal courts have made mixed decisions about the PPACA. Courts in Michigan, Florida, and New Jersey all ruled that the act was constitutional. A court in Virginia, however, declared in December 2010 that the act violated the commerce clause. Michael Landauer writing in a December 13, 2010, article in the *Dallas Morning News* noted that the Virginia decision was conservative judicial activism. He did not believe that made the decision wrong, however. Instead, he argued, "judicial activism is usually just the judiciary doing its job" by determining whether a law is constitutional.

Given the differing lower court decisions, the final decision as to the constitutionality of the PPACA will probably rest with the US Supreme Court.

The remainder of this chapter looks further at the commerce clause and discusses judicial activism in relation to other issues, including abortion, gay marriage, and gun control.

> *"If Congress can regulate this under the Commerce Clause, then it can regulate virtually anything—and the Federal Government is no longer one of limited and enumerated powers."*

Judicial Activism Has Dangerously Expanded the Interstate Commerce Clause

Thomas Sowell

Thomas Sowell is an economist, author, and a senior fellow at the Hoover Institution at Stanford University. In the following viewpoint, he argues that the Supreme Court made the wrong decision in a case involving the medicinal use of marijuana in California. The court said that the federal government could prosecute those who sold marijuana even though the state had legalized such sales. Sowell argues that the interstate commerce clause allows the federal government to regulate only trade between states, not trade within a single state. He says that expanding the commerce clause as the Supreme Court has done is unconstitutional and dangerously increases federal power.

As you read, consider the following questions:

1. According to Sowell, what does the Tenth Amendment to the Constitution say?

2. How did the Supreme Court authorize the vastly expanded powers of the federal government in 1942?

3. What did Clarence Thomas say would result if Congress could regulate California's medical marijuana program?

The Supreme Court's recent decision [June 2005] saying that the federal government can prosecute those using marijuana for medical purposes, even when state laws permit such use, has been seen by many as an issue of being for or against marijuana. But the real significance of this decision has little to do with marijuana and everything to do with the kind of government that we, our children, and our children's children are going to live under.

Marijuana and the Commerce Clause

The 10th Amendment to the Constitution says that all powers not granted to the federal government belong to the states or to the people.

Those who wrote the Constitution clearly understood that power is dangerous and needs to be limited by being separated—separated not only into the three branches of the national government but also separated as between the whole national government, on the one hand, and the states and the people on the other.

Too many people today judge court decisions by whether the court is "for" or "against" this or that policy. It is not the court's job to be for or against any policy but to apply the law.

The question before the Supreme Court was not whether allowing the medicinal use of marijuana was a good policy or a bad policy. The legal question was whether Congress had the

John Cox and Allen Forkum, "Doobious," Cox & Forkum, June 7, 2005. www.coxand forkum.com. Copyright © 2005 by Cox & Forkum. Reproduced by permission.

authority under the Constitution to regulate something that happened entirely within the boundaries of a given state.

For decades, judges have allowed the federal government to expand its powers by saying that it was authorized by the Constitution to regulate "interstate commerce." But how can something that happens entirely within the borders of one state be called "interstate commerce"?

Back in 1942, the Supreme Court authorized the vastly expanded powers of the federal government under Franklin D. Roosevelt's administration by declaring that a man who grew food for himself on his own land was somehow "affecting" prices of goods in interstate commerce and so the federal government had a right to regulate him.

No Limits on Federal Power

Stretching and straining the law this way means that anything the federal government wants to do can be given the magic la-

67

bel "interstate commerce"—and the limits on federal power under the 10th Amendment vanish into thin air.

Judicial activists love to believe that they can apply the law in a "nuanced" way, allowing the federal government to regulate some activities that do not cross state lines but not others. The problem is that Justice Sandra Day O'Connor's nuances are different from Justice Antonin Scalia's nuances—not only in the medical marijuana case but in numerous other cases.

Courts that go in for nuanced applications of the law can produce a lot of 5 to 4 decisions, with different coalitions of justices voting for and against different parts of the same decision.

A much bigger and more fundamental problem is that millions of ordinary citizens, without legal training, have a hard time figuring out when they are or are not breaking the law. Nuanced courts, instead of drawing a line in the sand, spread a lot of fog across the landscape.

Justice Clarence Thomas cut through that fog in his dissent when he said that the people involved in this case "use marijuana that has never been bought or sold, that has never crossed state lines, and that has had no demonstrable effect on the national market for marijuana."

Instead of going in for fashionable "nuance" talk, Justice Thomas drew a line in the sand: "If Congress can regulate this under the Commerce Clause, then it can regulate virtually anything—and the Federal Government is no longer one of limited and enumerated powers."

In short, the kinds of limitations on the power of the national government created by the Constitution are being nuanced out of existence by the courts.

Ironically, this decision was announced during the same week when Janice Rogers Brown was confirmed to the Circuit Court of Appeals. One of the complaints against her was that she had criticized the 1942 decision expanding the meaning of "interstate commerce." In other words, her position on this was the same as that of Clarence Thomas—and both are anathema to liberals.

"Clearly the Supreme Court is struggling to appropriately define the meaning of the Commerce Clause, not engaging in Judicial Activism."

Defining the Commerce Clause Does Not Constitute Judicial Activism

Matthew Provance

Matthew Provance is a lawyer. In the following viewpoint, he discusses the commerce clause, which allows the federal government to regulate interstate commerce. Provance argues that the expansion of the commerce clause is not due to judicial activism. Instead, he says, justices can legitimately disagree on how to apply the commerce clause. He argues that the long and variable case history of the commerce clause shows the court struggling with a difficult legal problem. He concludes that calling liberals "activists" in this context is misleading political rhetoric.

As you read, consider the following questions:

1. According to Provance, how did Thomas Jefferson, James Madison, and Roger Williams view the free exercise clause?

Matthew Provance, "Electing Justices in 2008, or, Ranting About the Commerce Clause," *The Sentinel*, March 7, 2008. Copyright ©2008 by The Ogden Newspapers Inc. Reproduced by permission.

2. In what cases does Provance say that the court scaled back the meaning of the commerce clause?

3. How did Antonin Scalia vote in the Supreme Court case involving Congress's power to regulate medicinal marijuana use?

This [viewpoint] is written in response to the January 23, 2008, *Sentinel* article . . . in which author Sean Martin expressed his disapproval of the United States Supreme Court's "Judicial Activism" over the last 180 years in defining the meaning of the Commerce Clause of the Constitution. Since its inception, the Supreme Court has struggled to determine the extent of Congress's power to govern conduct by both corporate entities and individual actors under its vague enumerated ability to "regulate commerce."

Originalists vs. Activists

The article portrayed the Commerce Clause debate as one between "Originalists," which the author defined as those who interpret the Constitution only as it was written and understood by the Framers, and "Judicial Activists," which the author defined as those who interpret the Constitution dynamically in the context of contemporary legal and societal concepts. Ostensibly, Martin's article is supposed to be about the importance of electing a president who will appoint Supreme Court justices who possess sound legal principles. In reality, it's a misinformed rant about the Commerce Clause; a hard sell on the author's equally misinformed overarching principles of constitutional interpretation.

Originalists are a small but vocal minority in the legal community. As a doctrine, Originalism can be attractive because of its clear application and elegant simplicity: The direct language of the Constitution and the Framers' intent are the only sources of inquiry. However, Originalism is, in my opinion, fatally flawed by that same simplicity. Often, the plain language of the Constitution is inconclusive. In the case of the Commerce Clause, the limit of Congress's power to "regulate commerce" is not inherently clear. Moreover, as there was no version of the *Congressional Record* in 1787, sometimes there is little definitive proof of how the Framers actually interpreted the words they drafted. Finally, Originalism severely downplays or outright rejects (depending on the variation of Originalism adhered to) the additional principle that we should interpret the Constitution in light of today's society and contemporary common-law principles.

For an anecdotal example, consider the Framers' view of the Free Exercise Clause (U.S. Const. Amend. I: "Congress shall make no law . . . prohibiting the free exercise [of religion]"). Thomas Jefferson's writings indicated that he viewed this language as a guarantee of freedom from institutionalized religion of any kind. James Madison, on the other hand, believed that the free exercise of religion would guarantee the boisterous presence of religion in daily life, encouraged by a multitude of sects free to practice within America. Finally, Roger Williams, a lesser-known Framer, saw the Free Exercise Clause as a protection of institutionalized religion from state influence, but not assistance: He viewed government action in support of religion as perfectly acceptable. Oftentimes the intent of the Framers is neither consistent nor dispositive when interpreting the Constitution. Despite these legitimate criticisms, Originalists like Martin tend to dismiss those that don't subscribe to their view as incompetents with liberal agendas. This type of dismissal is completely unwarranted, especially when supported by a very questionable analysis of the Commerce Clause and its history.

The Commerce Clause in Flux

My first problem with Martin's article is that it designates everything inconsistent with the principles of strict Originalism as "Judicial Activism," which has become in large part a de-

Justice Antonin Scalia Argues for Regulating Marijuana Under the Commerce Clause

Congress has undertaken to extinguish the interstate market in Schedule I controlled substances [the most dangerous drugs], including marijuana. The Commerce Clause unquestionably permits this. . . . To effectuate its objective, Congress has prohibited almost all interstate activities related to Schedule I substances. . . . Congress's authority to enact all of these prohibitions of intrastate controlled-substance activities depends only upon whether they are appropriate means of achieving the legitimate end of eradicating Schedule I substances from interstate commerce.

By this measure, I think the regulation [that is, the federal law outlawing medical marijuana use within a state] must be sustained. Not only is it impossible to distinguish "controlled substances manufactured and distributed intrastate" from "controlled substances manufactured and distributed interstate," but it hardly makes sense to speak in such terms. Drugs like marijuana are fungible [easily exchangeable] commodities. As the Court explains, marijuana that is grown at home and possessed for personal use is never more than an instant from the interstate market—and this is so whether or not the possession is for medicinal use or lawful use under the laws of a particular State.

Antonin Scalia,
concurrence in Gonzales v. Raich,
June 6, 2005. www.law.cornell.edu.

rogatory term thrown at judges whose rulings align with liberal ideologies. There is no such line in the sand when it comes to interpreting the Constitution, and to imply such simply injects politics into what is largely a bona fide legal question. At this point, Martin was pushing his agenda, and as a student of the law with an ardent distaste for politics, it irritated me. His contention that Originalism is mandated in Art. V (conferring exclusive power to Congress to alter the text of Constitution) and Amend. X (leaving powers not enumerated in the Constitution to the states) borders on the absurd. The same type of conclusory reasoning undermines Martin's discussion of the Commerce Clause.

While the Court's present interpretation of the Commerce Clause, which gives Congress power (subject to individual rights) to regulate any conduct that "substantially affects" interstate commerce is certainly a dynamic interpretation, dismissing it as "Judicial Activism" is simply not appropriate. Judicial Activism is, by definition, the expansion or protection of individual rights along social or political—and not legal—values. Usually we cry "Judicial Activism!" when the Court clearly and suddenly departs from established precedent. This is not the case with the Commerce Clause. The meaning of "regulate commerce" has been in transition for at least 180 years.

In 1824, *Gibbons v. Ogden* interpreted the Commerce Clause narrowly, to be extended somewhat by *Lochner v. New York* in 1905 and, admittedly, drastically by *NLRB [National Labor Relations Board] v. Jones & Laughlin Steel Corp.* (1937) and *Wickard v. Filburn* (1942). If that was the end of the story, perhaps a charge of Judicial Activism would be appropriate, though untimely, given that *Wickard* was decided over 60 years ago. But the Court scaled back the reach of the Commerce Clause in *US [United States] v. Lopez* (1995) and *US [United States] v. Morrison* (2000), only to subsequently extend it again with *Gonzales v. Raich* (2005). Clearly, the Supreme Court is struggling to appropriately define the meaning of the Commerce Clause, not engaging in Judicial Activism.

Political Propaganda

Finally, Martin's reliance on conservative justices as bastions of Originalism is misguided, at least when it comes to the Commerce Clause. While he praises recent additions John Roberts and Samuel Alito as "exceptional" (whatever that means), their track records in the lower courts indicate that while they may take a more limited interpretation of the Commerce Clause, they fall far short of a strict Originalist construction. As for Antonin Scalia, who might be described as almost an Originalist, he cast the swing vote in *Raich*, upholding Congress's power to regulate marijuana grown for personal medicinal use. In a concurring opinion, he justified such authority by an overhung-market theory substantially similar to that applied in *Wickard*. In Martin's world, perhaps only Clarence Thomas remains as a loyal torchbearer, which begs the question: Do you really want Clarence Thomas as your only supporter?

I wrote this response to [Martin's 2008 article] because I felt compelled to expose what I saw as political propaganda masquerading as legal analysis. The validity of the Court's stance on the Commerce Clause is certainly open to debate and a persuasive argument can be made that at present it reaches so far as to violate the Constitution. However, dismissing the status of the Commerce Clause as "Judicial Activism" and hurling broad generalizations oversimplifies the issue and misses the point: We define the meaning of our Constitution according to reasoned judgment, not through cheap scare tactics.

> "[Justice Elena] Kagan's anti-gun poten-
> tial is only one symptom of what gun
> rights advocates see as a broader di-
> lemma on the bench."

Judicial Activism Unjustly Restricts Gun Rights

Dave Workman

Dave Workman is senior editor of Gun Week *and a former
member of the National Rifle Association's board of directors. In
the following viewpoint, he argues that judges are often preju-
diced against gun owners and move to pass laws that unfairly
restrict gun use. He points in particular to recently appointed
Supreme Court justice Elena Kagan, who Workman says is a serious danger to gun owners. He also notes that judicial decisions
that protect wolves and other big-game animals from hunters are
unreasonable and dangerous.*

As you read, consider the following questions:

1. Why does Workman say that the sentencing of Cortez L.
   Montgomery was proper?

2. According to Judge Bender, who are the only people
   who should be allowed to have handguns?

3. According to Workman, why will Donald W. Molloy not find friends around hunting camps in Montana or Idaho?

Thursday's [August 5, 2010's] confirmation of Elena Kagan as the 112th justice to serve on the U.S. Supreme Court was one more signal that the court system, because of the people elected or appointed to the bench, is in serious trouble if not completely off the tracks, if one listens to the critics.

We have already discussed [in an earlier article] how this affects Evergreen State [Washington State] gun owners, and how it just might become an issue in the fall re-election bid by Sen. Patty Murray.

Kagan Will Hurt Gun Rights

The National Rifle Association's [NRA's] top guns—executive vice president Wayne LaPierre and chief lobbyist Chris Cox—weighed in with a serious objection; not unexpected, considering NRA's opposition to Kagan, but not so important as what the Brady Campaign's [an anti-gun group] Paul Helmke said. LaPierre and Cox issued a warning, but the Brady Campaign's remarks amounted to the proverbial "brick upside the head" for the firearms community. There are some 90,000 NRA members in Washington State, and today they're not a very happy lot.

The Brady Campaign was "proud to endorse" Kagan, according to the statement. The group is giddy to have an associate justice on the high court who "recognizes that reasonable gun regulations can save lives." Cases now filed in Chicago, North Carolina, New York and Maryland, and pending in California are aimed at defining what gun regulations are reasonable, and Kagan's views on that are not likely to square with those of, say, a member of the Washington Arms Collectors.

Bellevue's Alan Gottlieb, founder and executive vice president of the Second Amendment Foundation and chairman of the Citizens Committee for the Right to Keep and Bear Arms, is going to be busy for the foreseeable future. Fresh from his organization's Second Amendment victory in *McDonald v. City of Chicago* [a case that struck down Chicago city gun restrictions], there will be no "resting on his laurels."

It is not only Kagan's confirmation that has firearms owners fearful and bracing for battle. Kagan's anti-gun potential is only one symptom of what gun rights advocates see as a broader dilemma on the bench.

Perhaps the most egregious example in recent days comes from a lower state-level court in Columbus, Ohio. Last week, Common Pleas Judge John F. Bender sentenced one of two men involved in the shooting of a third man at a bar last November to three years in prison. It was a proper sentence, because Cortez L. Montgomery was a felon in possession of a gun in a prohibited place—a business where liquor is served—but the judge went overboard, revealing a prejudice that does not belong on the bench, the Buckeye Firearms Association implied.

Judicial Prejudice Against Firearms

"If I had my way," Judge Bender stated, according to the *Columbus Dispatch* story, "handguns would be illegal for everyone in this society except police officers. It destroys society."

Speaking of destroying society, a former Los Angeles County sheriff's deputy—one of those people Judge Bender would exclusively trust with a handgun—is on his way to prison for four years for attempting to smuggle drugs into a Castaic, CA, jail where he worked. His story was detailed by the *Los Angeles Times*, which reported that ex-lawman Peter Paul Felix, was busted in October 2008 while carrying heroin, methamphetamine and marijuana.

Maybe Judge Bender is thinking about a recently fired Fort Lauderdale, Fla., cop who had falsified his time cards to collect overtime, and in one case reported by the Broward-Palm Beach *New Times* and *Sun Sentinel* newspapers, he "failed to respond to another officer's call for backup." That call was to a retirement home, and the veteran cop, identified as Rick Burn, allegedly refused to respond, suggesting that the call involved some "senile old people."

Was Judge Bender alluding to the decorated Minneapolis cop who, according to the St. Paul *Pioneer Press*, was indicted by a federal grand jury for allegedly kicking a juvenile suspect in the head in July 2008 during an arrest at a city park? This case sounds eerily familiar with a situation in Seattle earlier this year in which an officer is caught on video kicking an innocent man, after which a female officer kicks him in the leg. The FBI is investigating.

Would Judge Bender trust the [former] Collier County, Fla., sheriff's deputy who was fired for harassing a woman who is now married to the former deputy's ex-husband? This female deputy reportedly harassed the woman while on duty, apparently an offshoot of a custody dispute involving the deputy and her ex-hubby.

Would Judge Bender hand a gun to either of the two Washington County, Tenn., sheriff's deputies who were cited in federal court for public nudity, possession of alcohol in a prohibited area and public intoxication?

Judge Bender may, or may not, hold a candle to King County Judge Judith Eiler for hijinks with a gavel, but at least it is *not* being reported that—while she was apparently verbally abusive to people in her courtroom—Eiler ever launched an anti-gun tirade from the bench. Eiler gets several days off. Judge Bender's is up in January 2011, and it appears the Buckeye Firearms Association is going to keep reminding its members about his philosophical leanings.

Judges Protecting Wolves

Speaking of judges, a federal judge in Montana—Donald W. Molloy of the District Court for the District of Montana—will not find any friends around hunting camps this fall in Montana or Idaho. On Thursday, he ruled that grey wolves in both states must be protected same as they are in Wyoming and elsewhere. Wolves in both states were de-listed, and last year hunting seasons on the big predators were opened to the shrill hysteria of environmentalists.

For those who think the petition to ban lead from hunting ammunition . . . is a threat to traditional hunting, allowing wolf packs to continue expanding is going to be equally devastating, according to the Rocky Mountain Elk Foundation [RMEF]. The Montana-based RMEF issued a blistering criticism of Judge Molloy's ruling that asserts the judge "has opened a door for perhaps the greatest wildlife management disaster in America since the wanton destruction of bison herds over a century ago."

"When federal statutes and judges actually endorse the annihilation of big game herds, livestock, rural and sporting lifestyles—and possibly even compromise human safety—then clearly the Endangered Species Act as currently written has major flaws," said David Allen, RMEF president and CEO in a press release. "We have already begun contacting the congressional delegations of Idaho, Montana and Wyoming to ask for an immediate review of this travesty—and reform of the legislation that enabled it."

RMEF is now calling on Congress to change the Endangered Species Act. Locally, Washington State hunters are furious, and the ruling is getting some heated reaction on the Hunting Washington Forum.

If one listens to gun owners and hunters, that's not the only thing in need of change. Judiciary philosophy could use an overhaul as well.

> *"The Court's approach to the text [of the Second Amendment] . . . is surely an unusual approach for judges to follow."*

The Expansion of Gun Rights Is a Dangerous Example of Judicial Activism

John Paul Stevens

John Paul Stevens served as a justice of the Supreme Court from 1975 to 2010. In the following viewpoint, he argues that the Second Amendment was intended to secure the right of militias to bear arms, not the right of individuals to do so. He points to the language of the amendment itself and to the debates about the Second Amendment at the time of its framing as evidence for his interpretation. He says that the Supreme Court majority is wrong to use the Second Amendment to strike down gun control regulations. He concludes that the judges are not following the original intent of the framers, but are instead taking it upon themselves to make new law.

As you read, consider the following questions:

1. What does Stevens say was the first major federal fire-arms law?

2. What two state Declarations of Rights does Stevens say protected civilian use of firearms?

3. What does Stevens say is the meaning of the term "bear arms"?

Guns are used to hunt, for self-defense, to commit crimes, for sporting activities, and to perform military duties. The Second Amendment plainly does not protect the right to use a gun to rob a bank; it is equally clear that it *does* encompass the right to use weapons for certain military purposes. Whether it also protects the right to possess and use guns for nonmilitary purposes like hunting and personal self-defense is the question presented by this case. The text of the Amendment, its history, and our decision in *United States v. Miller*, (1939), provide a clear answer to that question.

The Second Amendment and Militias

The Second Amendment was adopted to protect the right of the people of each of the several states to maintain a well-regulated militia. It was a response to concerns raised during the ratification of the Constitution that the power of Congress to disarm the state militias and create a national standing army posed an intolerable threat to the sovereignty of the several states. Neither the text of the Amendment nor the arguments advanced by its proponents evidenced the slightest interest in limiting any legislature's authority to regulate private civilian uses of firearms. Specifically, there is no indication that the Framers of the Amendment intended to enshrine the common-law right of self-defense in the Constitution.

In 1934, Congress enacted the National Firearms Act, the first major federal firearms law. Upholding a conviction under that Act, this Court held that, "[i]n the absence of any evidence tending to show that possession or use of a 'shotgun having a barrel of less than eighteen inches in length' at this time has some reasonable relationship to the preservation or efficiency of a well-regulated militia, we cannot say that the Second Amendment guarantees the right to keep and bear such an instrument." The view of the Amendment we took in *Miller*—that it protects the right to keep and bear arms for certain military purposes, but that it does not curtail the Legislature's power to regulate the nonmilitary use and ownership of weapons—is both the most natural reading of the Amendment's text and the interpretation most faithful to the history of its adoption.

Since our decision in *Miller*, hundreds of judges have relied on the view of the Amendment we endorsed there; we ourselves affirmed it in 1980. . . . No new evidence has surfaced since 1980 supporting the view that the Amendment was intended to curtail the power of Congress to regulate civilian use or misuse of weapons. Indeed, a review of the drafting history of the Amendment demonstrates that its Framers *rejected* proposals that would have broadened its coverage to include such uses.

The opinion the Court announces today [June 26, 2008] fails to identify any new evidence supporting the view that the Amendment was intended to limit the power of Congress to regulate civilian uses of weapons. Unable to point to any such evidence, the Court stakes its holding on a strained and unpersuasive reading of the Amendment's text; significantly different provisions in the 1689 English Bill of Rights, and in various 19th-century state constitutions; post-enactment commentary that was available to the Court when it decided *Miller*; and ultimately, a feeble attempt to distinguish *Miller* that places more emphasis on the Court's decisional process than on the reasoning in the opinion itself.

Even if the textual and historical arguments on both sides of the issue were evenly balanced, respect for the well-settled views of all of our predecessors on this Court, and for the rule of law itself, would prevent most jurists from endorsing such a dramatic upheaval in the law. As Justice [Benjamin N.] Cardozo observed years ago, the "labor of judges would be increased almost to the breaking point if every past decision could be reopened in every case, and one could not lay one's own course of bricks on the secure foundation of the courses laid by others who had gone before him." . . .

The text of the Second Amendment is brief. It provides: "A well-regulated Militia, being necessary to the security of a free State, the right of the people to keep and bear Arms, shall not be infringed."

Three portions of that text merit special focus: the introductory language defining the Amendment's purpose, the class of persons encompassed within its reach, and the unitary nature of the right that it protects.

A Well-Regulated Militia Is Necessary to the Security of a Free State

The preamble to the Second Amendment makes three important points. It identifies the preservation of the militia as the Amendment's purpose; it explains that the militia is necessary to the security of a free state; and it recognizes that the militia must be "well regulated." In all three respects it is comparable to provisions in several state Declarations of Rights that were adopted roughly contemporaneously with the Declaration of Independence. Those state provisions highlight the importance members of the founding generation attached to the maintenance of state militias; they also underscore the profound fear shared by many in that era of the dangers posed by standing armies. While the need for state militias has not been a matter of significant public interest for almost two centuries, that fact should not obscure the contemporary concerns that animated the Framers.

The parallels between the Second Amendment and these state declarations, and the Second Amendment's omission of any statement of purpose related to the right to use firearms for hunting or personal self-defense, is especially striking in light of the fact that the Declarations of Rights of Pennsylvania and Vermont *did* expressly protect such civilian uses at the time. Article XIII of Pennsylvania's 1776 Declaration of Rights announced that "the people have a right to bear arms for the defence *of themselves* and the state," §43 of the Declaration assured that "the inhabitants of this state shall have the liberty to fowl and hunt in seasonable times on the lands they hold, and on all other lands therein not inclosed." And Article XV of the 1777 Vermont Declaration of Rights guaranteed "[t]hat the people have a right to bear arms for the defence *of themselves* and the State." The contrast between those two declarations and the Second Amendment reinforces the clear statement of purpose announced in the Amendment's preamble. It confirms that the Framers' single-minded focus in crafting the constitutional guarantee "to keep and bear arms" was on military uses of firearms, which they viewed in the context of service in state militias.

The preamble thus both sets forth the object of the Amendment and informs the meaning of the remainder of its text. Such text should not be treated as mere surplusage, for "[i]t cannot be presumed that any clause in the Constitution is intended to be without effect."

The Court today tries to denigrate the importance of this clause of the Amendment by beginning its analysis with the Amendment's operative provision and returning to the preamble merely "to ensure that our reading of the operative clause is consistent with the announced purpose." That is not how this Court ordinarily reads such texts, and it is not how the preamble would have been viewed at the time the Amendment was adopted. While the Court makes the novel suggestion that it need only find some "logical connection" between the preamble and the operative provision, it does acknowledge that a prefatory clause may resolve an ambiguity in the text. Without identifying any language in the text that even mentions civilian uses of firearms, the Court proceeds to "find" its preferred reading in what is at best an ambiguous text, and then concludes that its reading is not foreclosed by the preamble. Perhaps the Court's approach to the text is acceptable advocacy, but it is surely an unusual approach for judges to follow.

"The Right of the People"

The centerpiece of the Court's textual argument is its insistence that the words "the people" as used in the Second Amendment must have the same meaning, and protect the same class of individuals, as when they are used in the First and Fourth Amendments. According to the Court, in all three provisions—as well as the Constitution's preamble, Section 2 of Article I, and the Tenth Amendment—"the term unambiguously refers to all members of the political community, not an unspecified subset." But the Court *itself* reads the Second Amendment to protect a "subset" significantly narrower than the class of persons protected by the First and Fourth Amendments; when it finally drills down on the substantive meaning of the Second Amendment, the Court limits the protected class to "law-abiding, responsible citizens." But the class of persons protected by the First and Fourth Amendments is *not* so limited; for even felons (and presumably irresponsible citizens as well) may invoke the protections of those constitutional provisions. The Court offers no way to harmonize its conflicting pronouncements.

The Court also overlooks the significance of the way the Framers used the phrase "the people" in these constitutional provisions. In the First Amendment, no words define the class of individuals entitled to speak, to publish, or to worship; in that Amendment it is only the right peaceably to assemble, and to petition the Government for a redress of grievances,

Justice Stephen Breyer on the Second Amendment

The majority's conclusion [in striking down Washington, DC, gun ban] is wrong for two independent reasons. The first reason is that set forth by Justice Stevens—namely, that the Second Amendment protects militia-related, not self-defense-related, interests. These two interests are sometimes intertwined. To assure 18th-century citizens that they could keep arms for militia purposes would necessarily have allowed them to keep arms that they could have used for self-defense as well. But self-defense alone, detached from any militia-related objective, is not the Amendment's concern.

The second independent reason is that the protection the Amendment provides is not absolute. The Amendment permits government to regulate the interests that it serves. Thus, irrespective of what those interests are—whether they do or do not include an independent interest in self-defense—the majority's view cannot be correct unless it can show that the District's regulation is unreasonable or inappropriate in Second Amendment terms. This the majority cannot do.

Stephen Breyer,
dissent in District of Columbia v. Heller,
June 26, 2008.

that is described as a right of "the people." These rights contemplate collective action. While the right peaceably to assemble protects the individual rights of those persons participating in the assembly, its concern is with action engaged in by members of a group, rather than any single individual. Likewise, although the act of petitioning the Government is a right that can be exercised by individuals, it is primarily collective in nature. For if they are to be effective, petitions must involve groups of individuals acting in concert.

Similarly, the words "the people" in the Second Amendment refer back to the object announced in the Amendment's preamble. They remind us that it is the collective action of individuals having a duty to serve in the militia that the text directly protects and, perhaps more importantly, that the ultimate purpose of the Amendment was to protect the states' share of the divided sovereignty created by the Constitution.

As used in the Fourth Amendment, "the people" describes the class of persons protected from unreasonable searches and seizures by Government officials. It is true that the Fourth Amendment describes a right that need not be exercised in any collective sense. But that observation does not settle the meaning of the phrase "the people" when used in the Second Amendment. For, as we have seen, the phrase means something quite different in the Petition and Assembly Clauses of the First Amendment. Although the abstract definition of the phrase "the people" could carry the same meaning in the Second Amendment as in the Fourth Amendment, the preamble of the Second Amendment suggests that the uses of the phrase in the First and Second Amendments are the same in referring to a collective activity. By way of contrast, the Fourth Amendment describes a right *against* governmental interference rather than an affirmative right *to* engage in protected conduct, and so refers to a right to protect a purely individual interest. As used in the Second Amendment, the words "the people" do not enlarge the right to keep and bear arms to encompass use or ownership of weapons outside the context of service in a well-regulated militia.

"To Keep and Bear Arms"

Although the Court's discussion of these words treats them as two "phrases"—as if they read "to keep" and "to bear"—they describe a unitary right: to possess arms if needed for military purposes and to use them in conjunction with military activities.

As a threshold matter, it is worth pausing to note an oddity in the Court's interpretation of "to keep and bear arms." Unlike the Court of Appeals, the Court does not read that phrase to create a right to possess arms for "lawful, private purposes." Instead, the Court limits the Amendment's protection to the right "to possess and carry weapons in case of confrontation." No party or *amicus* [friend of the court] urged this interpretation; the Court appears to have fashioned it out of whole cloth. But although this novel limitation lacks support in the text of the Amendment, the Amendment's text *does* justify a different limitation: the "right to keep and bear arms" protects only a right to possess and use firearms in connection with service in a state-organized militia.

The term "bear arms" is a familiar idiom; when used unadorned by any additional words, its meaning is "to serve as a soldier, do military service, fight." It is derived from the Latin *arma ferre*, which, translated literally, means "to bear [*ferre*] war equipment [*arma*]." One 18th-century dictionary defined "arms" as "weapons of offence, or armour of defence," and another contemporaneous source explained that "[b]y *arms*, we understand those instruments of offence generally made use of in war; such as firearms, swords. . . . By *weapons*, we more particularly mean instruments of other kinds (exclusive of firearms), made use of as offensive, on special occasions." Had the Framers wished to expand the meaning of the phrase "bear arms" to encompass civilian possession and use, they could have done so by the addition of phrases such as "for the defense of themselves," as was done in the Pennsylvania and Vermont Declarations of Rights. The *unmodified* use of "bear arms," by contrast, refers most naturally to a military purpose, as evidenced by its use in literally dozens of contemporary texts. The absence of any reference to civilian uses of weapons tailors the text of the Amendment to the purpose identified in its preamble. But when discussing these words, the Court simply ignores the preamble.

The Court argues that a "qualifying phrase that contradicts the word or phrase it modifies is unknown this side of the looking glass." But this fundamentally fails to grasp the point. The stand-alone phrase "bear arms" most naturally conveys a military meaning *unless* the addition of a qualifying phrase signals that a different meaning is intended. When, as in this case, there is no such qualifier, the most natural meaning is the military one; and, in the absence of any qualifier, it is all the more appropriate to look to the preamble to confirm the natural meaning of the text. . . .

The Amendment's use of the term "keep" in no way contradicts the military meaning conveyed by the phrase "bear arms" and the Amendment's preamble. To the contrary, a number of state militia laws in effect at the time of the Second Amendment's drafting used the term "keep" to describe the requirement that militia members store their arms at their homes, ready to be used for service when necessary. The Virginia military law, for example, ordered that "every one of the said officers, noncommissioned officers, and privates, shall constantly *keep* the aforesaid arms, accoutrements, and ammunition, ready to be produced whenever called for by his commanding officer." . . .

This reading is confirmed by the fact that the clause protects only one right, rather than two. It does not describe a right "to keep arms" and a separate right "to bear arms." Rather, the single right that it does describe is both a duty and a right to have arms available and ready for military service, and to use them for military purposes when necessary. Different language surely would have been used to protect nonmilitary use and possession of weapons from regulation if such an intent had played any role in the drafting of the Amendment.

No Individual Right for Citizens

When each word in the text is given full effect, the Amendment is most naturally read to secure to the people a right to use and possess arms in conjunction with service in a well-regulated militia. So far as appears, no more than that was contemplated by its drafters or is encompassed within its terms. Even if the meaning of the text were genuinely susceptible to more than one interpretation, the burden would remain on those advocating a departure from the purpose identified in the preamble and from settled law to come forward with persuasive new arguments or evidence. The textual analysis offered by respondent and embraced by the Court falls far short of sustaining that heavy burden. And the Court's emphatic reliance on the claim "that the Second Amendment . . . codified a *pre-existing* right," is of course beside the point because the right to keep and bear arms for service in a state militia was also a pre-existing right.

Indeed, not a word in the constitutional text even arguably supports the Court's overwrought and novel description of the Second Amendment as "elevat[ing] above all other interests" "the right of law-abiding, responsible citizens to use arms in defense of hearth and home."

> "The question of same-sex marriage is a purely political question, which has no meaningful legal component whatsoever."

Gay Marriage Should Be Decided Politically, Not by Judicial Activism

Paul Campos

Paul Campos is a professor of law at the University of Colorado at Boulder. In the following viewpoint, he argues that there is no constitutional basis on which to decide the question of whether same-sex marriage should or should not be legal. Thus, he says, when the Supreme Court rules on same-sex marriage, it will do so on the basis of the judge's political opinions. He concludes that relying on unelected officials to make these decisions is a bad idea and suggests that such issues should instead be left to legislatures.

As you read, consider the following questions:

1. According to Campos, which judges on the Supreme Court will vote to reverse *Perry v. Schwarzenegger*, and which will vote to uphold it?

2. What question does Campos say is almost completely constrained by the law, and what question does he say is almost completely unconstrained?

3. According to Campos, are arguments for and against judicial activism political questions, or are they legal questions? Why?

One of the acronyms spawned by the Internet is IANAL, which stands for "I am not a lawyer." This abbreviation is used by nonlawyers who participate in cyber-debates about what are supposedly questions of legal interpretation, such as, for example: Does the 14th Amendment prohibit states from refusing to recognize the legality of same-sex marriages? People who employ it are usually apologizing for their lack of legal expertise, while still hoping to contribute something useful to these debates.

Interpreting Justice Kennedy

Such apologies are unnecessary. The question of whether the 14th Amendment prohibits states from banning same-sex marriage is identical to the question of whether Justice Anthony Kennedy thinks the Supreme Court should require states to recognize same-sex marriage. This is because, when the Supreme Court eventually decides the outcome of *Perry vs. Schwarzenegger*, the case in which a federal judge this week [in August 2010] struck down a ban on gay marriage as unconstitutional, we can be almost certain that Justices [Samuel] Alito, [John] Roberts, [Antonin] Scalia, and [Clarence] Thomas will vote to reverse the outcome of the district court's ruling, while Justices [Stephen] Breyer, [Ruth Bader] Ginsburg, [Elena] Kagan, and [Sonia] Sotomayor will vote to uphold it.

That means that Kennedy, a once-obscure California lawyer who was put on the Supreme Court by Ronald Reagan, gets to decide if same-sex marriage becomes legal in the 45 states that currently do not recognize it. In other words, answering the question of whether laws prohibiting same-sex marriage are unconstitutional doesn't require one to interpret the Constitution—it merely requires that one interpret the likely behavior of Anthony Kennedy.

Now it's a standard feature of American politics to bewail this situation, while complaining about "judicial activism." According to this view, judges should not decide controversial questions of public policy by invoking vague pieces of constitutional language, such as the due process and equal protection clauses. (Both were employed in *Perry* by Judge Vaughn Walker, who found there was no "rational basis" for prohibiting same-sex marriages.)

These complaints are themselves vulnerable to a couple of criticisms. First, the complaining tends to be quite selective in an obviously partisan way. For example, it's very difficult to find conservative foes of "liberal activist judges" who are also willing to criticize the conservative wing of the Supreme Court when it invokes vague constitutional language to strike down campaign finance laws, or undermine affirmative action programs, or determine the outcome of a presidential election.

This, however, is a relatively minor quibble. To point out that people are inconsistent in their willingness to criticize judicial activism might reveal their hypocrisy, or stupidity, or both. But it is not necessarily a criticism of the argument that judges should avoid making activist decisions.

Law and Politics

A much deeper criticism is that the argument that judges should not decide controversial political issues by invoking vague constitutional language in expansive ways is *itself* every bit as much a political argument as the position it attacks. To see why this is so, consider two controversial questions: Should every state be represented in the Senate by two senators, regardless of population? And should federal tax rates be raised?

Any lawyer can tell you that the answer to the first question is almost completely constrained by the law, while the second is almost completely unconstrained. Every judge in America might believe, as I do, that the nonrepresentational structure of the Senate has become very bad for American politics, but every judge will tell you that the law requires every state to have exactly two senators, and that nothing can be done about this without first making a fundamental change to our law (by amending the Constitution).

The question of whether federal tax rates should be raised presents the reverse situation: Any judge will tell you that the law has nothing to say about the answer to that question. The first question is a question of law, while the second question is a question of politics—or, to put it another way the first question can become a question of politics only if we are willing to consider changing the law in a way that would make it one.

The invocation of vague constitutional language to decide controversial political issues—that is, judicial activism—consists precisely in treating political questions as if they were questions answered by the Constitution. Now opponents of judicial activism can offer all sorts of arguments why this is supposedly a bad thing. But note that none of these arguments will be legal arguments, in the sense that it's a legal argument to point out that the Constitution requires each state to have two senators.

Given that judicial activism is a central feature of our legal culture, all arguments against it (or for that matter in favor of it) are *political* arguments, and indeed are no different, in this respect, than arguments about what tax rates should be.

That said, it presents something of a challenge to construct an argument in favor of a system that gives a single unelected lawyer the power to determine the outcome of a great national controversy. Or, to put the question more directly: Is there a rational basis for the kind of judicial review that leads to conclusions such as that there is no rational basis for the law struck down in *Perry*?

This is another way of asking why Anthony Kennedy's views on whether same-sex marriage should be legalized ought to count more than those of all his 310 million fellow citizens combined. The question of same-sex marriage is a purely political question, which has no meaningful legal component whatsoever. (In other words, being a lawyer gives you no advantage over anyone else in getting the answer to this question right.) Indeed, perhaps the most plausible defense for this type of social engineering by judicial fiat is tradition—i.e., that's just how we've always done things in America. Which is rather ironic, given that this is exactly the same argument employed by the opponents of same-sex marriage.

Periodical and Internet Sources Bibliography

The following articles have been selected to supplement the diverse views presented in this chapter.

Wajahat Ali — "Judicial Activism: Playing with the Constitution," *Huffington Post*, September 12, 2008. www.huffingtonpost.com.

David Codrea — "National Parks Gun Ruling Is Judicial Activism, Not Justice," Examiner.com, March 21, 2009. www.examiner.com.

Sherrilyn A. Ifill — "Judicial Activism from the Right," *The Root*, January 24, 2010. www.theroot.com.

Michael Kinsley — "Look Who's a Judicial Activist Now," Politico.com, December 7, 2010. www.politico.com.

Robert A. Levy — *"District of Columbia v. Heller*: What's Next?" Cato Unbound, July 14, 2008. www.cato.org.

Dahlia Lithwick — "A Private Affair: The New Jersey Gay Marriage Decision Isn't Activism," Slate.com, October 25, 2006. www.slate.com.

Ben Tarr — "Roe v. Wade a Classic Example of Judicial Activism," *Daily Campus*, September 12, 2008.

William J. Watkins Jr. — "Obamacare, the Constitution, and the Original Meaning of the Commerce Clause," *Christian Science Monitor*, December 21, 2010.

John Yoo — "The Commerce Clause and ObamaCare's Undoing," Ricochet.com, December 13, 2010. http://ricochet.com.

OPPOSING
VIEWPOINTS®
SERIES

CHAPTER 3

What Is the Relationship Between Public Opinion and Judicial Activism?

Chapter Preface

One of the main criticisms of judicial activism is that it is nondemocratic. Supreme Court justices and other federal judges are appointed, not elected. Therefore, the argument goes, they are not responsive to public opinion. Those who oppose judicial activism claim that policy decisions should be made by the people's elected representatives, not by unelected judges.

Most states, however, have made state judges directly responsible to the public. Eighty-seven percent of all state court judges in the United States are elected.

The election of judges is quite popular with the American people. A poll by the American Justice Partnership, reported in a July 15, 2008, article by *American Courthouse*, found that 75 percent of voters thought state Supreme Court justices should be elected, with only 21 percent believing that judges should be selected through a nonpublic merit selection process. "Support for judicial elections was remarkably stable among voters," the article reports, "even when presented with numerous arguments against it." The popularity of judicial elections seems linked to the public's desire to have a say in the justice process. "If you want judges to be responsive to public opinion, then having elected judges is the way to do that," noted Sean Parnell, the president of the Center for Competitive Politics, which opposes campaign finance regulation, as quoted in a May 25, 2008, *New York Times* article by Adam Liptak.

However, many critics worry about electing judges. In the same *New York Times* article, former Supreme Court justice Sandra Day O'Connor is quoted in opposition to the practice. "No other nation in the world [elects judges]," O'Connor argued, "because they realize you're not going to get fair and impartial judges that way."

In particular, opponents of elections are concerned that judges may be indebted to those who contribute to their campaigns. Businesses or individuals who know they have cases coming before a court may make large donations to a judge running in an election. If the judge wins, he or she may not be able to render an impartial verdict in a case involving a party who gave him or her millions of dollars. A particularly flagrant example of this problem occurred in West Virginia, where Justice Brent Benjamin, running for the Supreme Court of Appeals, received $3 million from Massey Energy Company. Massey was involved in a lawsuit with another company. Benjamin won the election, and when the case came before him, he ruled in favor of Massey. The case was eventually appealed to the Supreme Court, which ruled in 2009 that Benjamin should have recused himself—that is, he should have stepped aside and left the decision to the others on the court. In his majority opinion for the Supreme Court, Justice Anthony Kennedy explained, "We conclude that there is a serious risk of actual bias—based on objective and reasonable perceptions—when a person with a personal stake in a particular case had a significant and disproportionate influence in placing the judge on the case by raising funds or directing the judge's election campaign when the case was pending or imminent."

Given these problems, some commentators have argued that there is a need to balance voters' desire for judicial elections with concerns about campaign contributions and fairness. Some states have already taken steps in this direction. In Texas, for instance, judges can accept campaign contributions, but not the very large amounts that created the conflict of interest in the West Virginia case. Still, a September 26, 2009, editorial in the San Angelo *Standard-Times* argued that more should be done. The paper recommended an initial appointment followed by periodic retention elections, so that the initial competence and impartiality of judges can be assured while voters can still have a say in the process. "Impartiality by judges is critical to a judicial system," the paper concluded. "So is the public's confidence in that the system isn't biased at the outset."

The viewpoints in this chapter further examine the relationship between public opinion, the judiciary, and judicial activism.

| "On the big issues, over time, the Court tends to come into line with public opinion."

Public Opinion Shapes Judicial Actions

Barry Friedman and Jeffrey Rosen

Barry Friedman is a professor of law at New York University; Jeffrey Rosen is the legal affairs editor of the New Republic. *In the following viewpoint, the authors argue that the Supreme Court generally aligns with public opinion over time and is very cautious about going against the legislative branch. The authors point to Supreme Court history to show that the court rarely challenges the legislative and executive branches, and that, when it does, it tends to lose. On the basis of this history, the authors argue that the conservative court led by Chief Justice John Roberts is unlikely to overturn the Democratic agenda of President Barack Obama.*

As you read, consider the following questions:

1. What do the authors say happened in the case *Marbury v. Madison*?

2. According to the authors, what percentage of the country agreed with the court's decision in *Brown v. Board of Education of Topeka*?

3. Why do the authors believe Justices Scalia and Kennedy would not vote to overturn health care reform?

Moments after Justice John Paul Stevens announced his intention to retire from the Supreme Court, Republican senators warned President Barack Obama not to appoint a judicial activist to replace him. Senator Orrin Hatch promised Obama "a whale of a fight if he appoints an activist to the court" and Senator Mitch McConnell warned that "Americans can expect Senate Republicans to make a sustained and vigorous case for judicial restraint and the fundamental importance of an evenhanded reading of the law."

The Court Is Cautious

But Hatch and McConnell's definition of "judicial activism" is topsy-turvy. When most people talk about judicial activism, they mean judges reaching out to strike down laws. But according to Hatch and McConnell, judges are activist if they *refuse* to strike down federal laws that Republicans oppose. Hatch voted against the health care mandate and, after he lost that fight, supported a lawsuit filed by 13 state attorneys general that asks the courts to strike down the individual mandate as unconstitutional. When McConnell lost the fight against the McCain-Feingold campaign finance bill [also known as the Bipartisan Campaign Reform Act], he successfully crusaded for the Supreme Court to strike the law down. In other words, on the most pressing national disputes of our day—from campaign finance to health care reform and financial reform—conservatives are embracing the very definition of judicial activism they spent the past 40 years denouncing, asking unelected judges to reverse their defeats in the political arena and all the while redefining this strategy as judicial restraint.

The political opportunism of these conservative activists is not surprising: Liberals during the Warren Court era [referring to the years from 1953–1969, when Earl Warren was chief justice] also relied on courts to hand them victories that eluded them in the political arena. Of course, during the Warren era, activism usually meant asking the Supreme Court to bring a few state outliers into line with a national consensus—on racial discrimination, for example. By contrast, Roberts Court-era [referring to the Supreme Court under Chief Justice John Roberts] conservatives are urging unelected judges to strike down landmark federal laws that passed over their objections, at least some of which command broad national support.

How will the Supreme Court respond to these attempts to enlist it in a war with the president and Congress? If history is any predictor, the justices won't be interested in a sustained assault. As both of us have written in recent books, on the big issues, over time, the Court tends to come into line with public opinion. Think here of gay rights, women's rights, and abortion. And when the Court has wandered outside the mainstream—on issues like the death penalty or economic regulation—it has quickly retreated after encountering resistance from the public, Congress, or the president. The Court, in other words, is very sensitive to the possibility of backlash against its actions; and if anything, the heated reaction to its recent decision striking down campaign finance restrictions on corporations is only likely to make it more so.

The Roberts Court Will Not Go Too Far

Despite the fact that this relationship between the Court and public opinion is now broadly accepted by people on both sides of the political spectrum, there are strident voices on the right and the left who are determined to deny this descriptive claim. Some of them have recently attacked us, and misconstrued our arguments about the way the Court behaves.

Additionally, they combine denial of how the Court *does* act with prescriptions for how it *should*. On the right, conservative defenders of judicial activism who view the courts as the last stand against perceived federal tyranny, such as *National Review Online* contributor Matthew Franck, are attempting to rewrite history and claim that courts can and should resist the president and Congress. On the left, some liberals, such as *New Republic* contributor Justin Driver, nostalgic for the judicial heroics they imagined in the Warren era, are (surprisingly enough) encouraging the courts to do precisely what conservatives want: embrace activism in the interest of protecting minorities in the face of determined national majorities.

We understand the impulse, on the left and the right alike, to resist the crude claim that justices do nothing more than follow the election returns. But while we are confident that public opinion constrains the justices somewhat, neither of us has *ever* argued that the justices should or do simply bow to the polls.

Our historical claim is more nuanced, and it is clearly borne out by the evidence. Don't take our word for it alone. Chief Justice Roberts himself has acknowledged in interviews that the justices are concerned about the legitimacy of the Court and reluctant to decide cases in ways that will imperil that legitimacy. His predecessor, William Rehnquist, made a similar point, explaining that the justices live in the world and are influenced by the same forces that affect the rest of us.

All of the reported leading names on President [Barack] Obama's shortlist to replace Justice Stevens—Merrick Garland, Elena Kagan, and Diane Wood—are stellar candidates, with broad support among conservative and liberal academics, who would undoubtedly oppose conservative efforts to reverse their political defeats. But replacing Justice Stevens will not alter the present conservative composition of the Court. So the question remains: Will we see a return to the constitutional conflicts of the 1930s, when the Supreme Court launched an assault on FDR's [Franklin D. Roosevelt's] New Deal, until he struck back by threatening to pack the Court. Anything is possible, but in the end, we are skeptical. A little realism about the Court suggests that Chief Justice Roberts is likely to balk at the siren calls of the conservative activists and decline to go very far down this fraught path.

Jefferson and Marshall

Hoping to bolster the conservative case for judicial activism, Matthew Franck has written a critique of [Jeffrey] Rosen [one of this viewpoint's authors] that exhibits not only a misunderstanding of history but also unrealistic hopes about what the justices will be able to do for the conservative struggle against President Obama and the regulatory state.

Franck takes issue with Rosen's claim that, in fights between the president and the Court, "it's almost always the president who prevails." To rebut the claim, Franck employs three historical gotchas. But each of Franck's examples actually proves the opposite of what he suggests.

Take the historic face-off [in the early 1800s] between Thomas Jefferson's Republican Party and the Supreme Court led by the Federalist John Marshall. Franck claims that the legendary chief justice was not fazed by Jefferson's attacks. "Was there ever any sign that Marshall's judicial decision-making was the least bit affected by the expostulations of Thomas Jefferson?" Franck asks. The answer, as it happens, is yes.

Before Jefferson took office, the lame-duck Federalists packed the judiciary with their loyalists by creating a number of new federal circuit courts and District of Columbia justice of the peace positions. When Jefferson's secretary of state, James Madison, failed to deliver the commission to one of the new justices of the peace, William Marbury, Marbury sued Madison. Justice Marshall then used the case to arrogate to the Supreme Court the power of judicial review. Sound familiar? No doubt, but this narrative leaves out the crucial backstory.

When the Supreme Court took Marbury's case and ordered Madison to explain his action, Jefferson's Republicans retaliated by abolishing all the new circuit-court judgeships. Everyone on both sides of the political divide knew this was a problem. The Constitution says that federal judges hold their office for life. But Republicans passed the legislation anyway, claiming a distinction between eliminating the office and firing the judge. The Republican move was quickly challenged, in a case called *Stuart v. Laird*. Knowing they were on thin constitutional ice, the Republicans then canceled the Supreme Court's next sitting so the Court couldn't rule on the constitutionality of the new law.

Then, when all this came before John Marshall's Court—after another national election that displayed continuing strong support for the Jeffersonian Republicans—the justices rolled over. *Marbury v. Madison* is famous today because, in the decision, Marshall asserted the power of the Court to review congressional acts for constitutionality. Indeed, Marshall also had strong things to say about the executive's obligation to act within the Constitution. But what most people aren't aware of is that it was nothing but a toothless lecture. Marshall ultimately avoided doing anything to protect Marbury's rights, by concocting an argument about why he didn't have jurisdiction to help. And, in handing Madison and Jefferson a victory, Marshall also arguably granted Congress a vehicle to strip the Court's jurisdiction whenever it wished. Thus, Marshall opted to preserve the prestige of the Court by accommodating the president, Congress, and the preponderance of popular opinion.

A History of Compromise

What about *Stuart v. Laird*, the case that was far more politically explosive, since, if the Court struck down the law abolishing the new circuit judgeships, it would have triggered an all-out revolt by Jeffersonians in Congress? It is difficult to believe Marshall really thought abolishing the judgeships was okay. When it came to resolving the case, Marshall simply recused himself, for reasons that are not entirely clear. What does seem evident is that he didn't want to be the one to have to run up the white flag. In *Stuart*, the Court actually *upheld* the removal from office of all the new Federalist judges—a dramatic expression of the Court's impotence in the face of a serious political threat.

Franck is equally wrong in his claim that "after a brief decade or so following the *Dred Scott [v. Sanford]* case, the Court was as strong as ever." *Dred Scott* was decided in 1857. In 1868, a Southern newspaper editor named McCardle, in federal custody, challenged the constitutionality of military rule of the South. The move endangered Congress's plan for bringing the South back into the Union. Congress responded by using the weapon Marshall had granted it and stripping the Supreme Court of its jurisdiction to hear the case. The Court's reaction, in this case involving the most basic of liberties, freedom from allegedly unconstitutional restraint? It bowed to Congress's action, recognizing another fight it could not win.

Lastly, Franck insists that the failure of Roosevelt's infamous Court-packing plan had nothing to do with the New Deal–era Court's decision to back down from its assault on FDR's programs. In the service of this assertion, he can only say that "we are pretty sure" Justice Owen Roberts, the key swing vote, was not influenced by the threat against the Court. Franck tries to bolster this case by denying that anything would have happened if the justices had proceeded to invalidate other social programs. "Woulda, coulda, shoulda. Sheer speculation based on nothing much, I'm afraid," he writes.

Nevertheless, after the Court's capitulation, newspapers screamed that the Court had switched. Editorialists and pundits indicated the plan as in deep trouble, a fact that polls confirmed. At the same time, congressional leaders assured FDR they could get something through Congress if only he'd limit the number of new justices he wanted. It was only FDR's stubbornness, and the untimely death of Senate Majority Leader Joseph Robinson, that brought the whole incident to a swift conclusion. If the Court, rather than capitulating, had struck down more New Deal measures in dramatic decisions that spring, it's hard to believe it would have emerged unscathed. A correspondent for the *Nation* reflected that, "had the court invalidated one Administration measure last term, nothing could have prevented the President from winning."

The Warren Court and the Public

From the left, Justin Driver has criticized our conception of the Court in a *New Republic* review of [this viewpoint's coauthor Barry] Friedman's book, *The Will of the People[: How Public Opinion Has Influenced the Supreme Court and Shaped the Meaning of the Constitution]*. This critique is plagued by similar misconceptions. Nostalgic for the activism of the Warren Court, Driver denies that the Court is in tether with public opinion. He also accuses Friedman of advocating that Supreme Court justices act with slavish subservience to public opinion: "Scholarship that encourages the justices to conduct themselves in such a conformist manner seems unwise and even dangerous, not least because the justices on the current Court seem particularly ill-equipped to divine the preferences of a majority of Americans."

This claim distorts, or even ignores, the book's thesis. *The Will of the People* never "encourages" the justices to be conformists or to "divine the preferences of a majority of Americans." It is, rather, a response to those who accuse the courts of wrongly interfering with the majority will. It argues that

Judicial Review and Democratic Institutions

Throughout history, the chief complaint against judicial review has been that it interferes with the right of the people to govern themselves. After the Supreme Court struck down yet another New Deal measure in 1936, the *New York Daily News*, the country's first tabloid, with a circulation at the time of well over one million, thundered: "We do not see how old judicial gentlemen . . . can forever be permitted to override the will of the people as expressed through the people's own elected Legislatures, Congress and President". . . . The president, the members of Congress, and the states' chief executives and legislators all are accountable to the people through regular elections. Not so the justices of the Supreme Court, who are appointed (not elected) and who—short of removal by impeachment, which has never happened—serve for life. Yet when the justices base a ruling on the Constitution, the country must live with that decision unless and until the Court reverses itself or the rare constitutional amendment is adopted. There is no overriding the Court otherwise.

Barry Friedman, The Will of the People:
How Public Opinion Has Influenced the Supreme
Court and Shaped the Meaning of the Constitution,
New York: Farrar, Straus and Giroux, 2009.

the justices ultimately are accountable to public opinion and that over the long haul, on the salient issues, Court decisions and public opinion come into line. The book concludes by insisting that the question we should be worrying about is whether the Court is capable of doing the same job that Driver wants it to do: protecting minority and constitutional rights.

In fact, Driver half-admits that he is making this analytical mistake, but presses on nonetheless. He writes that he recognizes the book is primarily "positive," which is to say it is a historical account of what the justices *have* done, and *why*, rather than a normative claim about what they *should* do. But, he insists, "the distinction between the positive and the normative cannot be drawn so neatly."

To the contrary, that distinction absolutely should be drawn, in the service of analytical clarity. Especially in this time of hyperbolic commentary on the Supreme Court, it is important not to ignore what political science and history have taught us about how the justices are likely to behave, as we are fashioning expectations about how they should behave. What is called for, on the right and left alike, is some realism when it comes to our perception of judicial decision making.

Take the Warren Court. Driver invokes the heroic tale of the Supreme Court's activism during the 1950s and 1960s, when it struck blows for racial justice, the rights of criminal defendants, and the downtrodden. It certainly did. But Driver neglects two salient points about that era. First, the justices' blows for constitutional liberty and equality were not so much courageous moves taken in the face of public opposition as they were legal interpretations that made sense as a product of their times. While forward-leaning, the Court's decisions were well within the broad mainstream of public opinion: During this period, there were many who sought desegregation and praised *Brown v. Board of Education [of Topeka]* when it came down (*Brown* was popular with 54 percent of the country), although of course there were opponents too. Second and more important to our thesis, *when the Court outstripped public opinion too greatly, it engendered a backlash that caused it to rein in its efforts.* Because ordering reapportionment of state legislatures was wildly popular, it happened quickly. By contrast, opposition to desegregation was so strong during this period that the lower courts had little success enforcing the mandate of *Brown*, and Congress had to step in with the Civil Rights Act of 1964. Similarly, much of the criminal-procedure revolution went down relatively easily because the public equated mistreating defendants with racial discrimination. But when the Court decided *Miranda v. Arizona*, eliminating confessions unless suspects were read their rights, at a time when crime rates were rising and rioting in urban ghettos was prominent, the public had had enough. Richard Nixon ran against the Warren Court, which had run squarely afoul of public opinion, and the Warren era ended.

Indeed, if anything illustrates how vulnerable an activist Court is to public backlash, it is the fate of *Miranda*. Driver writes that *The Will of the People* doesn't dwell long enough on *Dickerson v. United States*, the 2000 decision in which Chief Justice Rehnquist reaffirmed the long-embattled *Miranda* rule. In his telling, *Dickerson* shows how a courageous Court can lead the way, turning even unpopular rights into popular ones.

But likely the only reason Rehnquist wrote the majority opinion in *Dickerson* was because he lacked the votes to overrule *Miranda*, which he detested, and figured he could do damage control by staying in charge. Indeed, since then, both his Court and Chief Justice Roberts's have proceeded to quietly gut *Miranda*, until it becomes nothing but a façade. In 2004, for example, the Court held that although an un-*Mirandized* confession could not be admitted, any evidence found on account of it could! This very term, the Court has three more *Miranda* cases; in the two it has decided thus far, *Miranda* has been further whittled away. So much for heroics in defense of constitutional liberty.

To be fair, Driver makes several important observations. He is surely right that sometimes the Court can lead. Nevertheless, this is true only so long as the public is willing to be led, as the events subsequent to *Brown v. Board of Education* made clear. And, using *Brown* as an example, Driver makes the good point that sometimes a little political defiance can actually help the Court's image—though again, as *Brown* bears out, this can happen only so long as public opinion is roughly in tune and the justices ultimately prevail. (When they back down, as they did after the New Deal, the justices look weak). Defiance of the Court was common in the early 1800s, and it tended only to lead to more defiance.

The Democratic Agenda and the Roberts Court

Which brings us to the Roberts Court. Is it likely to stand in the way of Obama and the Democrats' agenda? What will happen, in particular, with health care [referring to the health care reform bill passed in 2010; some Republicans hoped to declare it unconstitutional]?

We aren't seers, and a lot can happen before any of this makes its way to the Court. But nothing we've seen—including January's decision in *Citizens United [v. Federal Election Commission*, which loosened campaign finance reform laws]— leads us to believe that the Court is likely to behave differently in the future than it has in the past.

Which means that the Court is going to be hesitant to launch a sustained challenge to the core of the Democratic agenda. And in the unlikely (but not impossible) event that it does decide to launch a sustained challenge, the justices will find themselves under attack in return as long as the Democrats still have popular support. If that happens, history suggests that such attacks on the Court will eventually precipitate some kind of judicial retreat.

It's possible, of course, that the Tea Party movement will grow and grow, support for health care reform will plummet in the polls, one or both houses of Congress will flip in the midterm elections, and Obama's popularity ratings will fall through the floor. Anything's possible. And if that all happens, the Court will have a lot more leeway to aggressively challenge

Democratic legislation. After all, the Supreme Court went after George Bush's Guantánamo [Bay detention camp] policy at a time of great skepticism concerning that administration's approach to the war on terror.

As for health care, it would be quite a trick for this Court to strike it down on the implausible claim that the mandate which requires all individuals to be insured exceeds congressional power. Even if five justices on the Roberts Court wanted to vote against the legislation, Justices [Anthony] Kennedy and [Antonin] Scalia are in a bind. They voted to uphold national power barring medicinal use of marijuana, on the grounds that Congress has control over a national market, and even purely "local" activity could affect that market. In light of that precedent, the constitutionality of health care reform seems like a no-brainer. Both of us believe that law matters to the justices, and we would be surprised to find that on that score, we're too naïve.

> *"This history suggests that a principled form of libertarian judicial activism— that is, one that consistently upholds individual rights while strictly limiting state power—is essential to the fight for a free society."*

Public Opinion Can Be Shaped for the Better by Judicial Activism

Damon W. Root

Damon W. Root is an associate editor of Reason *magazine and* Reason.com. *In the following viewpoint, he argues that judicial activism is consistent with the basic protection of individual rights. He believes that a libertarian form of judicial activism is essential for a free society. Root claims that for almost six decades judicial activism was associated with the protection of rights—specifically economic rights. The author concludes that this libertarian form of judicial activism is a basic requirement for a free society and will protect individuals against the "tyranny of the majority."*

Damon W. Root, "Unleash the Judges: The Libertarian Case for Judicial Activism," *Reason*, July 1, 2005. Reproduced by permission.

As you read, consider the following questions:

1. According to the viewpoint, what is the significance of Justice Stephen J. Field in regard to judicial activism?

2. What is Field's approach known as today, according to Root?

3. As stated by the viewpoint, who is Oliver Wendell Holmes?

Speaking to the Heritage Foundation in 1996 on the topic of "judicial activism," the conservative commentator Pat Buchanan denounced the Supreme Court as a "judicial dictatorship"; the Court's beneficiaries, he said, were "criminals, atheists, homosexuals, flag burners, illegal immigrants (including terrorists), convicts, and pornographers." In his influential 1996 book *Slouching Towards Gomorrah: Modern Liberalism and American Decline*, former federal appeals court judge Robert H. Bork declared that "the Supreme Court has usurped the powers of the people and their elected representatives." Dissenting from the majority in *Lawrence v. Texas* (2003), which nullified that state's anti-sodomy law, Supreme Court Justice Antonin Scalia argued that the Texas legislature's "hand should not be stayed through the invention of a brand-new 'constitutional right' by a Court that is impatient of democratic change."

Such views are widely shared on the right, where few subjects produce greater outrage than judicial activism, which conservatives blame for the forced imposition of liberal values on American society. But libertarians, who have frequently allied with conservatives in the effort to rein in the federal government, should not join their battle against the judiciary. There is no inconsistency between principled judicial activism and limited government.

Lincoln's Property-Rights Activist

For the better part of six decades, in fact, judicial activism was associated almost exclusively with the protection of economic rights, while its counterpart, judicial restraint, was the rallying cry of liberal reformers. Between Reconstruction and the New Deal, as the states began legislating a variety of new "progressive" regulations, it was judges acting in the name of private property and "liberty of contract" that "usurped" the power of the people, "invented" new rights, and gave birth to judicial activism as we know it today.

This history suggests that a principled form of libertarian judicial activism—that is, one that consistently upholds individual rights while strictly limiting state power—is essential to the fight for a free society. In fact, a genuinely libertarian jurisprudence would, in the words of the legal scholar Randy Barnett, "requir[e] the state to justify its statute, whatever the status of the right at issue." The real legal challenge facing libertarians isn't judicial activism; it is defending individual rights from the liberals and conservatives who seek to take our liberties away.

For a historical model, look to Supreme Court Justice Stephen J. Field. Appointed by Abraham Lincoln in 1863, Field sat on the Court for more than three decades, retiring in 1897 at age 81. In the words of biographer Paul Kens, Field was "the prototype for the modern judicial activist." He was among the first judges to create a body of legal authority by penning extensive dissenting and concurring opinions; he eagerly wielded the power of judicial review; he recognized few "political thickets" into which the courts should not tread. Nor did Field bind himself exclusively to legal precedent or to the text of the Constitution. Anticipating those 20th-century judges whose decisions draw on the political and social sciences, Field's opinions resound with such extra-constitutional sources as Adam Smith's *The Wealth of Nations* and the pre-

Where Gays Can Marry, as of April 2009

- ■ Same-sex marriage legal
- □ No prohibition in place
- ▨ Banned by state constitution
- ▨ Banned by state law

TAKEN FROM: Bill Meyer, "Vermont Legalizes Gay Marriage in Veto Override," *Plain Dealer* (Cleveland, OH), April 7, 2009. www.cleveland.com. Based on data from Human Rights Campaign, National Conference of State Legislatures.

cepts of natural law—the doctrine that man's rights derive from nature, not from human institutions.

Most important, Field advocated a groundbreaking jurisprudence of unenumerated natural rights. Through a number of creative and forceful opinions, particularly his dissents in the *Slaughter-House Cases* (1873) and *Munn v. Illinois* (1877), and his concurrence in *Butchers' Union Co. v. Crescent City Co.* (1884), Field worked to enhance judicial power, nullify popular legislation, and expand individual liberty under the 14th Amendment. . . .

Substantiating Due Process

Today, Field's approach is known as "substantive due process," referring to the idea that the due process clause guarantees more than just "procedural" rights and in fact secures all "substantive" or fundamental rights from violation as well. In other words, there is simply no official procedure, including the deliberative judgment of a legislative majority, that can legitimate the violation of inalienable rights.

Field's dread phrase "liberal construction" will no doubt send a few conservatives into apoplexy, since it so clearly foreshadows two of the Court's most controversial modern rulings. First, in *Griswold v. Connecticut* (1965), the Court held Connecticut's ban on the use of contraceptives to be a violation of the "zones of privacy" carved out by the specific guarantees of the Bill of Rights. Then, in *Roe v. Wade* (1973), the Court expanded the individual right to privacy to include the right to an abortion.

These decisions clearly fall within Field's interpretation. Individual rights, by nature and by necessity, he argued, require a broad or "liberal" scope if they are to have any real meaning. State power, by contrast, must be narrowly construed and strictly limited. Modern conservatives, by exalting the will of the majority over the liberties of unpopular minorities, have abandoned Field's natural rights-based approach for a constitutional vision that errs in favor of contested legislation. As we'll see, this doctrine of judicial restraint proved disastrous for individual rights in the 20th century.

In 1884 the butchers of New Orleans again provided Field with the opportunity to expound his sweeping vision of life, liberty, and property. Louisiana's new state constitution, passed in 1879, transferred the regulation of slaughterhouses from the statehouse to city hall. New Orleans responded by opening the business to limited competition, thus voiding the Crescent City Company's exclusive 25-year monopoly.

The issue before the Court in *Butchers' Union Co. v. Crescent City Co.*, therefore, was whether the state could impair its contractual obligations and rescind the privilege it had bestowed. The Court unanimously held that it could, since no legislature had the authority to limit the future exercise of its own police powers. Although he concurred with the ruling Field devoted the bulk of his opinion to restating his objection to the original monopoly and expanding his conception of liberty.

"Certain inherent rights lie at the foundation of all action," Field wrote. Among these "is the right of men to pursue happiness, by which is meant the right to pursue any lawful business or vocation, in any manner not inconsistent with the rights of others." This boldly libertarian position, which if followed would sweep away much state and federal legislation aptly demonstrates how judicial activism in defense of individual rights would limit the size and scope of government.

Although Field would die before his ideas fully entered the law, the tide had turned. In 1897, in the case of *Allgeyer v. Louisiana*, which overturned Louisiana's ban on mail-order insurance contracts sold by out-of-state companies, a unanimous Court explicitly recognized the right to pursue a calling, enshrining the broad 14th Amendment right to "liberty of contract." During the next three decades, the Court would selectively employ liberty of contract in several controversial cases to nullify popular state laws.

By far the most famous of these was *Lochner v. New York* (1905). In a decision still denounced for its judicial activism, the Court struck down New York's law setting maximum working hours for bakery employees on the grounds that it violated the liberty of contract protected by the 14th Amendment's due process clause.

"The act is not," Justice Rufus Peckham held for the majority, "within any fair meaning of the term, a health law." The legislature was plainly inspired by "other motives" than health or safety. Were the Court to uphold such an arbitrary state action, he continued, "there would seem to be no length to which legislation of this nature might not go."

Notably, *Lochner* was decided just nine years after *Plessy v. Ferguson* (1896), in which the Court upheld a Louisiana statute banning the sale of first-class railroad tickets to African Americans, permitting state-mandated segregation in public accommodations as long as the facilities for each race were "separate but equal." Although Field joined with the majority in this vile opinion (and remained uncharacteristically silent while doing so), *Plessy* clearly violates liberty of contract. As legal scholar Richard Epstein has written, "the statute sustained in *Plessy* was flatly inconsistent with laissez-faire principles. . . . *Plessy* represented the expansionist view of the police power that *Lochner* repudiated."

Individual Liberty vs. Good Government

It was precisely this repudiation of state power that motivated the attacks of *Lochner*'s many opponents. In his famous *Lochner* dissent, Justice Oliver Wendell Holmes lambasted his colleagues for enshrining "an economic theory which a large part of the country does not entertain." For Holmes, the deciding factor was the will of the majority, not individual rights. "I think that the word 'liberty' in the 14th Amendment," he explained, "is perverted when it is held to prevent the natural outcome of a dominant opinion, unless . . . the statute proposed would violate fundamental principles as they have been understood by the traditions of our people and our law."

This view, which became a central tenet of Progressive and New Deal–era liberalism, is precisely the approach now championed by Robert Bork, perhaps the leading conservative critic of the judiciary. The common denominator is that both liberals and conservatives will gladly sacrifice individual liberty to further their particular notions of "good government."

If Stephen Field is the first great champion of judicial activism, then Oliver Wendell Holmes is his nemesis, the first great advocate of judicial restraint. Appointed by Theodore Roosevelt in 1902, Holmes also sat for three decades, retiring in 1932 after exerting a vast and lasting influence, particularly on several key figures in Franklin Roosevelt's New Deal.

"I always say, as you know," Holmes once remarked, "that if my fellow citizens want to go to Hell I will help them. It's my job." That statement, perhaps more than Holmes or his supporters realize, perfectly captures the significant dangers inherent in judicial restraint. Consider, for instance, Holmes' dissent in *Meyer v. Nebraska* (1923), where the majority held that a state law banning foreign language instruction for young children, passed in the heat of the anti-German hysteria stirred up by World War I, violated the 14th Amendment's substantive guarantee of liberty. "I think I appreciate the objection to the law," Holmes explained, but "I am unable to say the Constitution of the U.S. prevents the experiment being tried."

Then there is Holmes' opinion for the majority in *Schenck v. United States* (1919), which upheld Woodrow Wilson's monstrous Espionage Act, permitting Congress to restrict and punish speech that obstructed the draft. This ruling sent Socialist leader Eugene V. Debs, among others, to federal prison, where he rotted for three years on the charge of exercising his First Amendment right to criticize the government. In both cases, Holmes' deference to the popular will placed him squarely against the fundamental rights of unpopular minorities.

Selective Rights

The obvious parallel here is to the Court's judicial restraint in *Korematsu v. United States* (1944), which upheld the [Franklin D.] Roosevelt administration's wartime internment of Japanese Americans. For those conservatives terrified at the thought of "judicial dictatorship," it's worth remembering that it was judicial restraint, not activism, that allowed these egregious violations of both fundamental rights and basic justice to occur.

Like Stephen Field before him, Oliver Wendell Holmes would not live to see his ideas become law. In 1937, five years after Holmes' death, the Supreme Court overturned *Lochner v. New York*, relying on the principle of judicial restraint to uphold a Washington State minimum wage law for women. Writing for the majority in *West Coast Hotel Co. v. Parrish*, Chief Justice Charles Evans Hughes rejected substantive due process and the notion of unenumerated rights. "The Constitution does not speak of freedom of contract," he declared. So long as an economic regulation is "reasonable in relation to its subject and is adopted in the interests of the community," the requirements of due process are met. To put it plainly, "the legislature is entitled to its judgment."

Conservative critics of judicial activism ought to celebrate this decision and the countless economic "reforms" that followed. Instead, many such critics, including Justice Scalia, still favor an active judicial role in defending property rights. Similarly, modern-day liberals remain firmly committed to the demise of liberty of contract while at the same time championing *Lochnerian* substantive due process for privacy and abortion rights.

Predictably, neither right nor left is eager to subject its selectively cherished rights to the will of the majority. And why would they? Majority rule, as James Madison pointed out in Federalist No. 10, is not always such a pretty thing. Fortunately, we possess inalienable rights that no majority may touch. Furthermore, as the Ninth Amendment says, "The enumeration in the Constitution, of certain rights, shall not be construed to deny or disparage others retained by the people." Stephen Field got that right in *Munn v. Illinois*: Individuals possess far more liberties than any constitution could possibly list.

A principled form of libertarian judicial activism, therefore, is clearly consistent with the basic requirement of a free society: the protection of individual rights against the tyranny of the majority.

> *"Judicial activism ... is a bad thing when the power of the court is used to overturn the clearly expressed will of the people."*

Judicial Activism Is Wrong When It Goes Against Public Opinion

Michael Laprarie

Michael Laprarie is an editor at the news website Wizbang. In the following viewpoint, he argues that judicial activism is justified in cases where public opinion is behind the court. He suggests that such was the case with the court's civil rights decisions. However, he argues, judicial activism should not be used to overturn the will of the people. He says that the federal court decision to make gay marriage legal in California is an example of bad judicial activism, since, he argues, Americans are overwhelmingly opposed to changing the definition of marriage to include gay unions.

As you read, consider the following questions:

1. What did Democrats in the South do that showed their political power, according to Laprarie?

2. According to Laprarie, what example of bad judicial activism did the civil rights movement produce?

3. What evidence does Laprarie provide that nationwide opinion is on the side of traditional marriage?

The recent kerfuffle over California's Proposition 8 "gay marriage ban" and its recent overturning by a federal appeals court got me thinking about the concept of judicial activism. It is a term that seems to be deliberately obfuscated on both sides of the political aisle.

Judicial Activism and Civil Rights

Conservatives routinely accuse liberal judges of using judicial activism to bypass the will of the people and enshrine controversial leftist policies into law. Liberals accuse conservatives of a desire to perpetuate bigotry and discrimination, pointing out that it was the activism behind landmark court cases like *Brown v. Board of Education [of Topeka]* that paved the way for the civil rights movement of the 1960s.

Is there such a thing as good judicial activism? In a word, "yes," and the civil rights movement is in fact a perfect example. After World War II, white Americans became much more aware of the discrimination faced by blacks, particularly in the Jim Crow South. After fighting a war to rid the world of tyranny, it seemed even more disturbing that the Land of the Free was keeping a significant portion of its own people from enjoying the rights and freedoms that were the foundation of our Constitution and Declaration of Independence.

Although many (particularly in the Deep South) strongly resisted efforts to end legalized segregation, a series of pivotal events including the Emmett Till murder and Rosa Parks' historic standoff with authorities aboard a Montgomery, Alabama, bus gradually convinced the nation at large that something was wrong.

But the political power of the Southern Democrats was very strong. In previous decades, they had twice defeated congressional antilynching legislation. President [Dwight] Eisenhower publicly opposed segregation, but history seemed to indicate that blacks could not count on Congress to pass legislation that would effectively end Jim Crow.

Undoubtedly it was the courts, through their rulings that compelled school districts in the South to begin the process of desegregation, that finally cracked the veneer of racism in America. Empowered by court-ordered desegregation and armed with the strategy of nonviolence (in direct contrast to the violent reaction of whites) the civil rights movement fully manifested itself in the early 1960s culminating in the 1964 Civil Rights Act and the 1965 Voting Rights Act.

Interestingly though, the civil rights movement also gave us a perfect example of *bad* judicial activism—court-ordered busing. In the late 1960s federal judges realized that racially segregated neighborhoods were the major contributing factor to lingering school segregation problems. In an ill-conceived effort to diversify the racial composition of schools, courts began to order school districts to bus students across town in order to achieve racial balance. These rulings proved to be extremely unpopular with blacks as well as whites. Wikipedia notes:

> Even though school districts provided zero-fare bus transportation to and from students' assigned schools, those schools were in some cases many miles away from students' homes, which often presented problems to them and their families. In addition, many families were angry about having to send their children miles to another school in an unfamiliar neighborhood when there was an available school a short distance away. The movement of large numbers of white families to suburbs of large cities, so-called white flight, reduced the effectiveness of the policy. Many whites who stayed moved their children into private or parochial schools; these effects combined to make many urban school

US Views on Gay Marriage, 2010

	Legal	Illegal
All	47	50
Democrat	60	39
Independent	50	48
Republican	27	69
Northeast	55	39
Midwest	48	50
South	37	61
West	57	41
Age 18–29	65	33
Age 30–64	47	51
Age 65+	30	66

TAKEN FROM: Jennifer Agiesta, "Post-ABC Poll: Views on Gay Marriage Steady, More Back Civil Unions," *Behind the Numbers Blog, Washington Post*, February 12, 2010. http://voices.washingtonpost.com.

districts predominantly nonwhite, reducing any effectiveness mandatory busing may have had.

The Will of the People

Judicial activism can be a good thing, if public opinion is in the process of aligning with the opinion of the court, and court rulings can be legitimately understood as a means necessary to overcome diminishing, though still powerful, pockets of resistance. But it is a bad thing when the power of the court is used to overturn the clearly expressed will of the people (such as a public referendum), or to circumvent democracy in the form of the legislative process.

All of this brings us back to Chief Judge Vaughn R. Walker's decision regarding California's Proposition 8 referendum.[1] This is clearly a case of bad judicial activism. The vote in California may have been close (52–48%), but nationwide opinion is clearly on the side of traditional marriage. In 2004, eleven states voted on legislation or constitutional amendments that would define marriage as a legal union between a man and a woman. Those questions passed with double-digit margins in all eleven states; the margin here in Oklahoma was 3:1, and Mississippi's referendum passed with a whopping 86% of the vote.

While the majority of Americans clearly support equal rights for LGBT [lesbian, gay, bisexual, and transgender] citizens, and a majority would also probably support secular same-sex civil unions or domestic partnerships, it is also very clear that a vast majority of Americans *DO NOT* support tampering with the traditional definition of marriage. Any attempt by courts to overrule the will of the people with respect to such deeply held beliefs will leave us fractured and bitter, just as the court-imposed legalization of abortion did, nearly 40 years ago [in the 1973 *Roe v. Wade* decision].

1. Michael Laprarie, "Some Thoughts About Judicial Activism," Wizbang.com, August 18, 2010. Copyright © 2010 by Wizbang.com. Reproduced by permission.

"Poll after poll has shown that the American people . . . embrace . . . the view that judges should be more like neutral umpires, saying what the law is and not what they think it should be."

The Public Opposes Judicial Activism

Wendy Long and Gary Marx

Wendy Long is counsel to the Judicial Crisis Network (JCN); Gary Marx is executive director of JCN. In the following viewpoint, they argue that President Barack Obama's Supreme Court nominee, Sonia Sotomayor, is a dangerous judicial activist. They say that her reliance on personal feelings and politics, rather than the law, to make decisions has made her unpopular. Instead, they argue, polls show that the public wants neutral judges who behave as umpires rather than activists.

As you read, consider the following questions:

1. What does the Zogby poll say about support for Sotomayor, according to the authors?

2. What nominee do the authors say was the only one to garner more opposition than Sotomayor?

3. What senators do the authors say plan to vote against a Supreme Court nominee for the first time in their careers?

A new Zogby/O'Leary Report poll confirms what JCN [Judicial Crisis Network, a conservative organization focused on Supreme Court confirmation battles] has been saying for a long time: The more the American public learns about Judge Sonia Sotomayor [President Barack Obama's first Supreme Court appointee], the more they will agree that she is a liberal judicial activist who will decide the "hard" cases based on personal politics and feelings.

The Public Opposes Sotomayor

According to the Zogby poll released Monday [July 27, 2009], less than half of Americans (49%) support Judge Sotomayor's confirmation and an equal number oppose it. Hispanic voters are roughly split on Sotomayor, 47% in favor and 43% against, while independent voters oppose her confirmation (55% to 44%) as do small business owners (52% to 42%).

Gun owners—who had considerable reason to oppose Judge Sotomayor after she refused to tell senators the right to bear arms is a "fundamental right"—oppose her confirmation by more than a 2-1 margin, 67% to 30%. [The poll was conducted July 21–24, surveyed 4,470 voters, and has a margin of error of plus or minus 1.5 percentage points.]

These and other poll results show an overwhelming level of opposition to a Supreme Court nominee who, at the time of her nomination, was expected by some to be a shoo-in because of her life story and background. As Gallup announced recently in an analysis of a separate poll, "[w]ith only 9% of Americans expressing no opinion about Sotomayor's fate, the lowest seen for any nominee, she now garners more opposition than any Supreme Court nominee of the past two decades, except for the unsuccessful Harriet Miers [a President George W. Bush appointee]."

In contrast, "[s]upport for [Samuel] Alito's confirmation grew after widely televised confirmation hearings," said Gallup, with 54% of Americans expressing support and only 30% opposing. A poll conducted by Gallup after the Senate confirmation hearings for [Chief Justice] John Roberts found that 60% of Americans supported his confirmation and only 26% opposed.

President Obama promised he would appoint a Supreme Court justice who would decide the "hard" cases by relying on personal feelings and politics. He fulfilled that promise by nominating Judge Sotomayor, whose record of speeches, law review articles, and judicial decisions demonstrates that she and President Obama are on the same page when it comes to liberal judicial activism.

A Lawless View of the Judiciary

Poll after poll has shown that the American people reject that lawless view of the judiciary, and that they embrace the rule of law and the view that judges should be more like neutral umpires, saying what the law is and not what they think it should be. Through the confirmation process, and the efforts of groups like JCN to bring much-needed attention to the process, the American people have now learned enough about Judge Sotomayor to conclude that she is unworthy of their endorsement because she rejects their traditional conception of the judicial role.

The public's views on this important issue are obvious, which is why Judge Sotomayor and her Democratic boosters went out of their way during her public hearings to pretend (incredibly) that they have discovered the virtue of judicial restraint and the rule of law. Senators Orrin Hatch and Charles Grassley today voted against the approval of a Supreme Court nominee for the first time in their long Senate careers. Their votes reflect the strong view of the American people in favor of judges ruling impartially based on the law, not on their personal views, experiences, and opinions. And though a final vote on the nomination has not been scheduled, already 18 senators have announced that they will vote against Judge Sotomayor—more than any Democratic Supreme Court nominee since 1916.

Despite her life story, the historic nature of her nomination as a female Hispanic, the support of a popular president and an overwhelmingly Democratic Senate, and widely publicized confirmation hearings during which she claimed to turn her back on decades of prior statements and writings, the public has not been fooled into supporting a judicial activist. To the contrary, efforts to educate the public and motivate thousands of Americans to get engaged in the battle over judicial philosophy are paying off; the cost of nominating and confirming judicial activists is the highest it has been in our lifetimes.

> "A vague notion about adherence to the
> Constitution is simply not going to get
> the rest of the country's blood boiling."

The Public Does Not Care About Judicial Activisim

Paul Waldman

Paul Waldman is a senior correspondent for the American Prospect *and the author of* Being Right Is Not Enough: What Progressives Must Learn from Conservative Success. *In the following viewpoint, he argues that Republicans use the phrase "judicial activism" to signal to their base that a judge supports the abortion rights granted in* Roe v. Wade. *Waldman says that most of the electorate finds the concept of "judicial activism" abstract and not relevant to their lives. Therefore, he concludes, conservative use of the phrase is self-defeating; the public cannot be persuaded to oppose a judge on the grounds that she is an activist.*

As you read, consider the following questions:

1. Why did George W. Bush reference the *Dred Scott* decision in a debate with John Kerry, according to Waldman?

2. According to Waldman, what percent of the public believes that *Roe* should not be overturned?

3. What should the appointment of a new Supreme Court
justice be occasion for, according to the author?

It is becoming clear that conservatives will be unable to tor-
pedo Sonia Sotomayor's nomination to the Supreme Court.
What is also becoming clear is that they're losing an opportunity to convince the public that their vision of the courts is
superior to that of progressives. And they have no one to
blame but themselves.

Even before President Barack Obama nominated Sotomayor, conservatives became incensed when Obama said that
"empathy" was a key virtue he looked for in a justice. Empathy, they charged, was nothing but a "code word" masking
Obama's true agenda. And these people know from code
words. In fact, their biggest problem in this debate is that so
much of the time, they themselves speak in code.

Granted, some of the attacks aimed at Sotomayor are
straightforward, albeit idiotic and tinged with the eternal
grievance of the subjugated white male. But these are mere
sidelights and considered by most of the Republicans in the
Senate with the power to actually hold up Sotomayor's nomination to be too dangerous to touch. They, along with many
of the conservative groups opposed to the nomination, are
sticking with the old standbys, particularly "judicial activism."

As has been noted many times before, a "judicial activist"
is a judge who makes a ruling you don't like. Those who have
attempted to quantify activism, by defining it as the propen-
sity to strike down laws or regulations, for instance, have
found that it's the conservative justices who are the most "activist." But the charge was always meant to be a dog whistle, a
signal that only certain people were supposed to understand.
To the conservative base, the charge that a judge appointed by
a Democrat was a judicial activist meant that he or she would

favor affirmative action, worker protections, equal rights for gays, the separation of church and state, and above all, *Roe v. Wade*. At the same time, the formulation was intended to say to the outside world that conservatives weren't concerned about particular outcomes at all but merely wanted the judiciary to stick to the law and the Constitution and not "legislate from the bench."

The problem with dog-whistle politics, however, is that it doesn't have the power to persuade those whose ears aren't attuned to the whistle. And anyone who will recoil in fear when told that Sonia Sotomayor is a "judicial activist" was opposed to her before they even knew who she was.

Conservatives have gotten so used to talking in code that they've forgotten who their audience is. Not that it hasn't been important for them in the past—for instance, in one of his debates with John Kerry in 2004, President George W. Bush said that he would pick Supreme Court justices who "would not allow their personal opinion to get in the way of the law," and as evidence for the wrong approach he cited *Dred Scott [v. Sanford]*, the 1857 case that upheld slavery. "That's a personal opinion. That's not what the Constitution says," Bush said. Observers found the reference a bizarre non sequitur, until the rest of us discovered that anti-choice activists often compare *Roe* to *Dred Scott*. Bush was sending a signal to conservative Christians: Worry not, my friends—I'll make sure that anyone I appoint to the Supreme Court will be a vote to overturn *Roe*.

But reassuring your supporters that you'll pick their kind of justice is not the same as persuading the broader American public that a president's nominee ought to be feared and hated. Those conservative Christian Republicans don't need to be persuaded to oppose Sotomayor—they'd oppose any nominee offered by a Democratic president. It's the rest of the country that needs persuading. And a vague notion about adherence to the Constitution is simply not going to get the rest of the country's blood boiling.

Even as their arguments fall flat, it's hard to blame Republicans for staying at such an abstract level. Their problem is that if they actually got specific, they'd be even less persuasive.

Nowhere is this more clear than when it comes *Roe v. Wade*. Think of the lengths Republican nominees have gone to conceal their opposition to the decision, refusing to even talk about it in their confirmation hearings. The most laughable case was Clarence Thomas, who told the Judiciary Committee with a straight face that not only did he have no opinion one way or another about *Roe*, he had never in his life even participated in a conversation about the most contentious Supreme Court decision of our time (once on the Court, Thomas urged overturning the case in *Planned Parenthood [of Southeastern Pennsylvania] v. Casey*, to no one's surprise). The two Republican nominees who followed Thomas did their best to imply that they might just uphold *Roe*. When asked about the case, both John Roberts and Samuel Alito talked at length about *stare decisis*, the doctrine that prior Supreme Court decisions should be respected. "There's nothing in my personal views based on faith or other sources that would prevent me from applying the precedents of the court faithfully under principles of *stare decisis*," Roberts said. Alito assured the committee he would approach any question on abortion with an "open mind." Virtually no one invested in the abortion debate believed either of them.

Why is this ridiculous charade necessary? For the same reason that conservative activists and politicians will never admit that what they mean by "judicial activist" is someone who supports *Roe*: because they know that they're on the wrong side of public opinion. A CNN poll taken two weeks ago asked whether people thought *Roe* ought to be overturned; 68 percent said no. Roberts and Alito certainly knew what they were doing; a CNN/*USA Today*/Gallup poll taken while the

Sonia Sotomayor

When President [Barack] Obama announced her nomination, on May 26th [2009], it was clear that Sotomayor—who, two weeks later, fractured her ankle running late at LaGuardia [Airport]—would be a different kind of Justice, someone a little more connected, as the White House kept reminding everyone, with "the real world." She was a *boricua* from the Bronx, a diabetic, a divorcée, a dental-bill debtor, a person who, the night before her investiture ceremony, belted out "We Are Family" in a karaoke bar at a Red Roof Inn. ("It was all Titi Sonia's idea," her cousin Marisol Gutierrez told *Latina*.) The financial-disclosure form that she filed with the Senate revealed that, in 2008, in a Florida casino, she had won $8,283 playing cards. [Justice Antonin] Scalia, a few years earlier, had become embroiled in a conflict-of-interest drama after going on a duck-hunting trip with Dick Cheney; Sotomayor once recused herself from a case because, she wrote, "I was a member of the BJ's Wholesale Club Inc." Whether her name was pronounced Soda-may-er (Senator Jeff Sessions), Soto-my-ur (Senator Richard Durbin), Soto-my-air (Senator Al Franken), or Soto-may-ay-or (Senator Tom Coburn), she cut a relatable figure. The Bronx congressman José Serrano said that, after her nomination, "people on the street would come running up to me and talk about 'Sonia,' like she's their cousin, or their niece."

Lauren Collins, "Number Nine," New Yorker, January 11, 2010. www.newyorker.com.

Alito nomination was pending asked, "Suppose that after his confirmation hearings you were convinced Samuel Alito would vote to overturn the *Roe v. Wade* decision on abortion. If that were the case, would you like to see the Senate vote in favor of Alito serving on the Supreme Court, or not?" Only 34 percent of respondents said they would want the Senate to confirm him, while 56 percent said they would not.

And what else is on the conservative judicial agenda? It may have been best described by Jeffrey Toobin in a *New Yorker* profile of Chief Justice John Roberts:

> "After four years on the Court, however, Roberts's record is not that of a humble moderate but, rather, that of a doctrinaire conservative. The kind of humility that Roberts favors reflects a view that the Court should almost always defer to the existing power relationships in society. In every major case since he became the nation's seventeenth Chief Justice, Roberts has sided with the prosecution over the defendant, the state over the condemned, the executive branch over the legislative, and the corporate defendant over the individual plaintiff. Even more than Scalia, who has embodied judicial conservatism during a generation of service on the Supreme Court, Roberts has served the interests, and reflected the values, of the contemporary Republican Party."

That's as good a summary of what conservatives want out of the Supreme Court as you'll find. It also points to why Sotomayor is likely to breeze through her hearings, regardless of the screeching from the likes of [Rush] Limbaugh and [Newt] Gingrich. Were Roberts's views on things like the scope of presidential power discussed at dinner tables and water coolers during his confirmation? Only in rarefied circles. The broader public never considered the possibility that Roberts could be an ideological extremist, not just because the Democratic opposition to his nomination was so anemic but because he seemed so, well, nice. Polite, thoughtful, good-looking in a forgetful, local weather guy kind of way, Roberts gently batted away questions from Democratic senators on his way to an easy confirmation. Compare him to Robert Bork [nominated in 1987 by Ronald Reagan, but not confirmed], he of the scowling visage and Mephistophelian goatee, who looked as if he could explode in anger at any moment.

And what is the public going to see in the Sotomayor hearings? An obviously well-qualified nominee, being questioned by a bunch of Republicans about "judicial philosophy" and "activism," abstract ideas with no apparent connection to people's lives. They won't be able to say what kind of rulings they're afraid Sotomayor might make and why she would be a threat. They won't argue that she'll be a vote to uphold *Roe*, or that she'll support workers like Lilly Ledbetter [the plaintiff in a 2007 employment discrimination suit] when they are discriminated against by their employers, or that she'll rule that the president's powers are not limitless. They will pretend to be investigating Sotomayor's record for sinister leanings, without ever admitting just what it is they hope to discover.

By repeating the mantra of "judicial activism" over and over, conservatives have made it easy for Sotomayor to respond. At some point in her confirmation hearings (probably more than once), some senator will ask her, "Judge, do you believe it's the job of a Supreme Court justice to apply the Constitution, or do you believe they should make the laws?" To which she will reply, "Senator, it's the job of the Supreme Court to apply the Constitution." Asked and answered. Since the "evidence" they have that Sotomayor is a secret activist is so pathetically thin, there won't be much more to say.

In a perfect world, the appointment of a new Supreme Court justice would be the occasion for a meaningful debate about the role the Court plays in our democracy and the different understanding of the Constitution, and justice itself, that the two parties hold. Alas, that is not the world in which we live. So we are treated to an endless argument about a single line, even a single *word* ("better") Sonia Sotomayor used in a speech eight years ago, alongside a series of increasingly ugly outbursts from the puffy blowhards of the right. They have certainly succeeded, for a brief moment anyway, in framing this debate around their own ugly identity politics. But when Republicans finally get the chance to question Sotomayor, they'll drone on and on about their opposition to "judicial activism." It's just about the only card they have to play. And it won't be enough.

> *"Learned liberal treatises on jurisprudence abound, justifying judicial activism on behalf of any number of ends."*

The Public Opposes Judicial Activism Because It Does Not Understand the Issue

Doug Bandow

Doug Bandow is a senior fellow at the Cato Institute and author of Beyond Good Intentions: A Biblical View of Politics. *In the following viewpoint, Bandow discusses the issue of judicial activism. Although he believes judges who intervene whenever necessary to promote liberal values and policies enact judicial activism incorrectly, he also believes that conservatives who reject any type of judicial activism "in the name of interpreting the Constitution" are also wrong. What does matter, notes Bandow, is the correct interpretation of the Constitution, even if judges do or do not support what they are interpreting.*

As you read, consider the following questions:

1. What courts were "merely following popular values," according to the viewpoint?

Doug Bandow, "Conservative Judges, Liberal Crisis," *American Spectator*, August 8, 2007. Reproduced by permission.

2. What does Bandow claim "fidelity to the Constitution" means?

3. As stated in the viewpoint, what should judges have in order to render impartial, well-reasoned decisions?

Judges are supposed to be liberals. Modern, big government liberals, not classical, individualistic liberals. But the current Supreme Court, complains Sen. Chuck Schumer (D-N.Y.), is "the most conservative in memory." It is "dangerously out of balance." Sen. Schumer is horrified that the Supreme Court justices are no longer promoting the usual left-wing political agenda.

What to do? The Senator declares that no additional Bush Supreme Court nominees should be confirmed "except in extraordinary circumstances" (presumably meaning that Laurence Tribe gets the nod).

Sen. Arlen Specter (R-Pa.), the prototypical Republican in Name Only, also is upset. In late July [2007], he announced his intention to review the testimony of Chief Justice John Roberts and Associate Justice Samuel J. Alito at their confirmation hearings. He doubts they "lived up" to their promises to respect legal precedents—that is, to preserve the liberal state created by past liberal jurists. Senate Majority Whip Richard J. Durbin (D-Ill.) suggested more thorough questioning of future nominees, since Justice Roberts's performance "has been in conflict with many of the statements he has made privately, as well as to the committee."

Another option being advanced by the left is to simply pack the Court with pliant nominees. Urges Jean Edward Smith of Marshall University: "If the current five-man majority persists in thumbing its nose at popular values, the election of a Democratic president and Congress could provide a corrective." Just add another justice or two, as proposed by Franklin Delano Roosevelt. (Of course, no commitment to precedent would be necessary at the confirmation hearings of these Democratic nominees.)

Washington is rife with awful arguments, shameless demagoguery, and flagrant hypocrisy, of course. But Smith's concern lest "a majority of Supreme Court justices adopt a manifestly ideological agenda" and plunge "the court into the vortex of American politics" is almost too hilarious to repeat. Apparently the [Chief Justice Earl] Warren and [Chief Justice Warren] Burger Courts were merely following popular values when they overturned decades and even centuries of precedent to transform sizable areas of constitutional law. When they turned the law into a matter of judicial preference rather than constitutional interpretation, they presumably did so in a nonideological and nonpolitical fashion.

The courts rewrote legislation involving abortion, welfare, racial discrimination, busing, law enforcement practices, church-state relations, private property seizures, and much more. Most of these cases involved the Supreme Court ruthlessly overriding popular preferences and democratic choices. In fact, that's what the courts are supposed to do—when the Constitution mandates that they do so. But modern liberal judicial philosophy is quite different: intervene whenever necessary to promote modern liberal values and policies. Reject judicial intervention whenever necessary to promote modern liberal values and policies.

No wonder those on the left are so upset with the Roberts Court. It sometimes acts as if constitutional provisions and legislative enactments should be interpreted as written and understood by those who enacted them. How antediluvian. How outrageous. How un-liberal!

Conservative Activists Just as Wrong

Conservative activists who denounce any judicial activism in the name of interpreting the Constitution also don't have it right. The problem is not judicial activism per se, but whether the Constitution is being properly interpreted.

In some cases, the nation's fundamental law demands that the courts act to implement its provisions. For instance, barring government from taking land except for a public use has no meaning if judges don't actually determine whether a particular taking is for a public use, and, if not, override the government's decision even if reached democratically. Vindicating the First Amendment means voiding laws backed by a popular majority if they violate the liberties protected.

Fidelity to the Constitution often means judges refusing to act, even if they doubt the wisdom of a particular executive or legislative policy. But honest judging requires jurists to intervene in other cases, even where they might support the law or practice at issue. As Founder James Madison explained, the judiciary was to be "an impenetrable bulwark against every assumption of power in the Legislative or Executive."

Judicial philosophy obviously matters. Here the right long has gotten the argument much more correct than the left. Conservatives can and do argue about exactly what "original intent" should constitute—I believe that constitutional and legislative provisions must be understood in terms of the political compromises from which they sprang. What did the voters and ratifiers as well as drafters believe to be true? That may not always be easily discoverable, of course. Nevertheless, constitutional (and legal) understandings must be rooted in what the provisions meant when enacted. Otherwise there is little to prevent courts from becoming mini-legislatures, enacting their preferences through shameless sophistry disguised as judicial opinions.

Learned liberal treatises on jurisprudence abound, justifying judicial activism on behalf of any number of ends. But all of these arguments lead to the same basic result: a much-expanded state built on the tenets of modern liberalism. Once the official meaning of law is cut loose from what its specific provisions were originally expected to mean, the only restraint on judges is their personal temperament. If the Constitution means what judges say it does, it means nothing at all. A court that can eviscerate the property takings clause, for instance, can eviscerate the First Amendment guarantees for free speech and religious liberty, and the Fourth Amendment's bar on unreasonable searches and seizures.

Although unbridled judicial activism is an unsatisfactory jurisprudential principle, the left has nowhere else to go because the Constitution is fundamentally, though not purely, a libertarian-conservative document. The nation's basic law is meant to constrain politics, to put many issues, centered around an expansive and expensive national government, out of bounds of the democratic process. In short, to be a liberal and believe in original intent is to be eternally frustrated.

After all, as Georgetown University Law Center professor Randy Barnett points out, the Constitution is best understood as establishing islands of government power in an ocean of individual rights. The former are not unimportant and the latter are not unlimited, but a fair reading of the Constitution yields a limited national state that accords high value to civil, economic, and political freedoms. The underappreciated Ninth as well as Tenth Amendments compel this conclusion.

Douglas T. Kendall of Community Rights Counsel and James E. Ryan of the University of Virginia School of Law rightly point out in a recent *New Republic* article that the Civil War altered the Constitution. Indeed, one can speak of America having two constitutions. Write Kendall and Ryan: "A federal government that began with powers that were 'few and defined' was awarded vast new powers to protect due process and equal protection. Conservatives may not like this, of course, but they should not be able to wish away these changes."

The post–Civil War amendments obviously expanded federal authority, but most obviously vis-à-vis the states, and for the purpose, most particularly, of ensuring that the newly freed slaves would be protected in the exercise of their traditional liberties. These amendments were not intended to provide the foundation for the 20th-century welfare/redistributionist/nanny state. Indeed, via the doctrine of "incorporation," that is, the application of the Bill of Rights to the states, backed by contemporaneous evidence indicating that supporters of the provisions desired this result, the post–Civil War amendments applied the Constitution's most explicit limitations on—authorizations of—federal power to states as well.

The Conundrum

So the problem recurs: How to create a liberal state via judicial interpretation when the nation's basic document bars creation of much of that state? This conundrum helps explain why the left seems even more oriented than the right towards results-oriented jurisprudence. This dilemma also explains liberal angst over preserving "precedent." Sen. Specter is upset about the abandonment of precedent not because he is concerned about stability in the law. All of the decisions which he seeks to preserve, most notably *Roe v. Wade*, upset prior decisions and settled law. Rather, he emphasizes precedent because he wants to preserve more recent court decisions ratifying the modern liberal state.

Even more so, leading Democrats fear that a more conservative court will dismantle the jury-rigged judicial justification for so many of today's expansive state. They talk precedent because that is their best argument to use against conservatives. Should liberals install a firm left-wing majority on the Supreme Court, all talk about precedent would instantly vanish.

The discussion would suddenly turn to the importance of judges vindicating the rights of those, namely liberals, who feel denied a fair opportunity to impose their agenda through the political process.

Should the Senate rigorously assess the qualifications of presidential nominees to the U.S. Supreme Court and the rest of the federal bench? Of course. Judges should have the temperament, integrity, and knowledge necessary to render impartial, well-reasoned, and fact-based decisions.

Moreover, their jurisprudence should base interpretation on fidelity to the meaning of the text when proposed, drafted, and enacted. The underlying political compromise will not always be obvious, and good people can differ in the application of even clear principles to complicated factual situations. Nevertheless, holding a result-based jurisprudence, whatever the particular end, should be grounds for rejection.

With the addition of Justices Alito and Roberts, the current Supreme Court has become more conservative. But left-wing activists have little credibility to complain, having thoroughly politicized the courts for decades. Today's conservative jurists still get a lot wrong, but almost any conservative jurisprudential philosophy is better than the result-oriented theories advocated by leading Democratic lawmakers.

Periodical and Internet Sources Bibliography

The following articles have been selected to supplement the diverse views presented in this chapter.

Emily Bazelon	"Supreme Courtship," *New York Times*, September 25, 2009.
Kellyanne Conway	"Key Findings from a National Survey of 800 Actual Voters," Federalist Society Website, November 5, 2008. www.fed-soc.org.
Justin Driver	"Why Law Should Lead," *New Republic*, April 2, 2010.
Orin Kerr	"What if the Public Doesn't Like Limited Government?" *Volokh Conspiracy*, January 28, 2008. http://volokh.com.
Mike Rappaport	"Supreme Court Legitimacy?" *The Right Coast*, January 25, 2008. http://rightcoast.typepad.com.
Jeffrey Rosen	"How the Election Affects the Court," *New Republic*, November 8, 2004.
Ilya Somin	"The Supreme Court's Approval Ratings and the Legitimacy of Judicial Review," *Volokh Conspiracy*, January 27, 2008. http://volokh.com.
Sol Wachtler and David Gould	"The Myth of Judicial Activism," Newsday.com, July 18, 2009. www.newsday.com.
David Weigel	"Conservatives Prep Dossiers, Polls for Court Fight," Washington Independent, May 7, 2009. http://washingtonindependent.com.

OPPOSING
VIEWPOINTS®
SERIES

CHAPTER 4

Is Judicial Activism an Issue in Other Countries?

Chapter Preface

In other countries, judicial activism raises many of the same issues as it does in the United States. On the one hand, activist judges may interfere with the legislative and executive powers, which are more directly responsible to the people. On the other hand, an active judiciary can be an important break on unfair or authoritarian actions by the other sectors of government.

In India, judicial activism has been seen much more positively than it has in the United States. Many commentators have applauded the active role of the judiciary, arguing that activism redresses injustices in the Indian system of government. For example, in a July 19, 2009, article on the MeriNews website, Jaspal Singh traces judicial activism in India back to the 1979 case of Indian politician Maneka Gandhi, who was denied a passport by the government of India. The Supreme Court of India in that case ruled against the government, expanding the Indian right to due process. Singh notes that the judiciary has continued to protect individual rights, sometimes against the wishes of the government. He concludes that "judicial activism has played an important role in protecting human rights. In other words, it has indeed proved to be a boon to the victims of arbitrary, illegal and unconstitutional actions of state as well as of public servants."

Abhinav Chandrachud, writing in a July 18, 2009, article in the *Hindu*, agrees that judicial activism has advanced important rights. He expresses concern, however, that the Indian judiciary may be overreaching. In particular, he points to a case in which the Supreme Court instructed the government to seek "an explanation of the steps taken by it to ameliorate the plight of Indian students in Australia, who have been facing racially motivated attacks." Chandrachud notes that the Supreme Court decision encourages "dialogue and transparency," but he suggests that it is also essentially unenforceable. As a result, he worries that it will delegitimize the judiciary.

Justice B.N. Srikrishna, writing in a 2005 article in *Law Resource India*, came out even more strongly against judicial activism. Srikrishna argues that judges should strive to be neutral arbiters, and warns that "in the name of judicial activism, modern-day judges in India have abandoned the traditional role of a neutral referee and have increasingly resorted to tipping the scales of justice in the name of 'distributive justice'. The legitimacy of such actions needs critical appraisement at the hands of the legal fraternity, even at the risk of unpopularity by swimming against the tide."

The viewpoints in this chapter examine debates about judicial activism in Canada and Pakistan.

> *"In all of these jurisdictions, activist judges have violated the common law, distorted the Constitution, and defied the express will of Parliament by writing same-sex marriage into law."*

Judicial Activism in Canada Is Undermining Democracy

Rory Leishman

Rory Leishman is an author and columnist for the Interim, London Free Press, *and* Catholic Insight. *In the following viewpoint, he argues that judicial activism has become a dangerous problem in Canada since the Charter of Rights and Freedoms was signed into law in 1982. He says that, for example, courts have ignored the will of Parliament and forced the acceptance of gay marriage. He concludes that the growing power of unelected judges threatens the rights and liberties of all Canadians.*

As you read, consider the following questions:

1. How did the Canadian Alliance attempt to limit the effect of judicial decisions on marriage and the natural family, according to Leishman?

2. In 2003, how did Ontario's chief justice reformulate the common-law definition of marriage?

3. What cardinal principle of democracy does Leishman say that judges violate when they create entitlements?

On 17 April 1982 the Canadian Charter of Rights and Freedoms was signed into law. In the meantime, Parliament and the provincial legislatures have also progressively broadened the scope of their respective human rights codes. Together, these radical innovations in the Canadian constitutional order were supposed to safeguard the human rights and fundamental freedoms of Canadians. But have these new laws succeeded? Or have they served as an excuse for human rights tribunals and the courts to undermine freedom, democracy, and the rule of law in Canada?

The Charter of Rights and Freedoms

Prior to the Charter, Parliament and the provincial legislatures were supreme—that is, they had virtually untrammelled authority to make, amend, and revoke laws within their respective spheres of legislative jurisdiction under the division of federal and provincial powers in the Constitution. Today, the Supreme Court of Canada reigns supreme over the legislative as well as the judicial process. Time and again over the past twenty years, unelected judges on this Court have issued guidelines on legislative policy to the democratically elected representatives of the people of Canada in what is supposed to be the legislative branch of government. On occasion, the Court has circumvented the democratic process altogether by changing the law on its own.

Consider, for example, the decision of the Supreme Court of Canada in *Vriend v. Alberta*, 1998. At issue in this case was a dispute between the administration of King's University College in Edmonton and Delwyn Vriend, an employee of the college who had mocked the school's Christian code of conduct by wearing a T-shirt emblazoned with a homosexual slogan. At the instigation of some indignant students, King's College fired Vriend. He appealed the dismissal, first to the Human Rights Commission of Alberta and then to the courts. Eventually, the case ended up before the Supreme Court of Canada. In a ruling on 2 April 1998, Canada's top court held that in dismissing Vriend for insubordinate behaviour, the college had violated the ban on discrimination on the basis of sexual orientation in the Alberta Human Rights, Citizenship, and Multiculturalism Act.

This was a remarkable ruling inasmuch as there was not, and never had been, any reference to sexual orientation in the Alberta human rights act. Indeed, the Supreme Court of Canada frankly acknowledged in its judgment in *Vriend* that the Alberta Legislature had repeatedly refused to proceed with Opposition demands that a provision on sexual orientation be incorporated into the province's human rights legislation. Likewise, there is not now, and never has been, any mention of sexual orientation in the Canadian Charter of Rights and Freedoms. Like the Alberta Legislature, the Parliament of Canada clearly rejected proposals to include any reference to sexual orientation in the Charter when it was adopted. But has the Supreme Court of Canada paid any heed to such unmistakable indications of the express will of elected representatives of the people in Parliament and the provincial legislatures? Not at all. First, in *Egan v. Canada*, 1995, the Court read sexual orientation into the equality rights provisions of section 15 of the Charter, and then, three years later in *Vriend*, the Court cited *Egan* as authority for a decision to flout the Legislature of Alberta by reading a ban on discrimination on the basis of sexual orientation into the Alberta human rights act.

Judicial Activism and Gay Marriage

In *M. v. H.*, 1999, the Supreme Court of Canada followed up on *Egan* and *Vriend* by decreeing that the denial of spousal benefits to same-sex couples under the Ontario Family Law

Act was inconsistent with the allegedly implicit equality rights of homosexuals in section 15 of the Charter to an extent that could not be demonstrably justified in a free and democratic society. Just five years earlier, the elected representatives of the people of Ontario had debated this same issue at the instigation of Ontario's attorney general, Marion Boyd. On behalf of the New Democratic Party government of Premier Bob Rae, she introduced a bill that proposed to give cohabiting gay and lesbian couples essentially the same rights and responsibilities in provincial law as common-law couples. The proposal met with a popular outcry so intense that backbenchers among Boyd's fellow New Democrats were moved to join with the Opposition in defeating the bill. Typically, the Supreme Court of Canada has paid no heed to this clear and deliberate expression of the will of the majority of the elected representatives of the people. However, instead of abruptly amending the law as in *Vriend*, the Court condescended in *M. v. H.* to give the Ontario Legislature six months to come up with a series of amendments ensuring that the spousal benefits and obligations of cohabiting same-sex couples are equivalent to those of heterosexual, common-law couples in the laws of Ontario. The Legislature promptly complied. Where Boyd failed, the Court succeeded in browbeating the elected legislators of Ontario into expediting passage of an omnibus bill that conferred spousal benefits upon same-sex couples under the Ontario Family Law Act and sixty-six other Ontario statutes. In short order, Parliament and the legislatures of every other province followed suit: They, too, meekly and promptly brought their laws into line with the discovery by the Supreme Court of Canada in *M. v. H.* that the Constitution of Canada mandates equal rights for homosexual and heterosexual couples in common-law relationships.

In an attempt to limit the adverse impact of *M. v. H.* on marriage and the natural family, the Canadian Alliance proposed a resolution in the House of Commons on 8 June 1999 declaring: "It is necessary, in light of public debate around recent court decisions, to state that marriage is and should remain the union of one man and one woman to the exclusion of all others, and that Parliament will take all necessary steps within the jurisdiction of the Parliament of Canada to preserve this definition of marriage in Canada." Prime Minister Jean Chrétien supported this Opposition resolution. And so did most of his Liberal Cabinet. In leading off debate for the government on the resolution, Justice Minister Anne McLellan avowed: "Let me state again for the record that the government has no intention of changing the definition of marriage or of legislating same-sex marriages." McLellan flatly rejected the contention of gay rights activists that homosexuals have the same right to marry as heterosexuals. She said: "I fundamentally do not believe that it is necessary to change the definition of marriage in order to accommodate the equality issues around same-sex partners which now face us as Canadians." She added: "Marriage has fundamental value and importance to Canadians and we do not believe on this side of the House that that importance and value is in any way threatened or undermined by others seeking to have their long-term relationships recognized. I support the motion for maintaining the clear legal definition of marriage in Canada as the union of one man and one woman to the exclusion of all others."

With the backing of most Liberal and Progressive Conservative members of Parliament, this Canadian Alliance resolution upholding the historic definition of marriage in the common law of Canada was adopted by the overwhelming margin of 216 to 55. Eight months later, Parliament and the Chrétien government reaffirmed their support for the traditional definition of marriage in the Modernization of Benefits and Obligations Act—the omnibus federal bill that was adopted pursuant to the *M. v. H.* ruling for the purpose of conferring equality rights on same-sex couples in some sixty-eight federal statutes. In an explanatory note, the federal Department of Justice explained that the changes in federal law effected by the act "will ensure that, in keeping with the Supreme Court of Canada decision in *M. v. H.* (May 1999), same-sex common-law couples have the same obligations and benefits as opposite-sex common-law couples and will provide them with the same access as other Canadian couples to social benefits programs to which they have contributed." A more abject parliamentary capitulation to the legislative will of the Supreme Court of Canada is hard to imagine, yet even in this act, Parliament made a point of reiterating in section 1.1: "For greater certainty, the amendments made by this Act do not affect the meaning of the word 'marriage,' that is, the lawful union of one man and one woman to the exclusion of all others."

No Respect for Parliament

Have the appeal courts of Canada paid any heed to these repeated expressions of parliamentary support for the traditional definition of marriage? Definitely not. On 1 May 2003 the British Columbia Court of Appeal decreed in *Barbeau v. British Columbia (Attorney General)*, 2003, that the common-law bar to same-sex marriage violates the equality rights of homosexuals in section 15 of the Charter. In reasons for the Court, Madame Justice Jo-Ann Prowse said that while she was disposed to reformulate the common-law definition of marriage as "the lawful union of two persons to the exclusion of all others," she had decided to suspend this remedy until 12 July 2004 "solely to give the federal and provincial governments time to review and revise legislation to bring it into accord with this decision."

Even this small courtesy to Parliament and the provincial legislatures was too much for the Ontario Court of Appeal. On 10 June 2003 a three-judge panel led by Ontario's chief justice, Roy McMurtry, abruptly declared in *Halpern et al. v.*

Canadian Charter of Rights and Freedoms

Whereas Canada is founded upon principles that recognize the supremacy or God and the rule of law:

Rights and freedoms in Canada

1. The Canadian Charter of Rights and Freedoms guarantees the rights and freedoms set out in it subject only to such reasonable limits prescribed by law as can be demonstrably justified in a free and democratic society.

Fundamental freedoms

2. Everyone has the following fundamental freedoms:

(*a*) freedom of conscience and religion;

(*b*) freedom of thought, belief, opinion and expression, including freedom of the press and other media of communication;

(*c*) freedom of peaceful assembly; and

(*d*) freedom of association.

Canadian Charter of Rights and Freedom,
Part I of the Constitution Act, 1982,
Canada Department of Justice,
http://laws.justice.gc.ca.

Attorney General of Canada et al., 2003: "We reformulate the common-law definition of marriage as 'the voluntary union for life of two persons to the exclusion of all others.'" By this means, the Court immediately granted same-sex couples the unprecedented right to marry in Ontario. Since then, courts in Manitoba, Newfoundland, Nova Scotia, Saskatchewan, Quebec, and the Yukon have done the same: In all of these jurisdictions, activist judges have violated the common law, distorted the Constitution, and defied the express will of Parliament by writing same-sex marriage into law.

In reaction to these illegitimate rulings, Parliament could have invoked its power under the notwithstanding clause of the Constitution to enact a bill reaffirming the traditional definition of marriage. Chrétien rejected this option. He abandoned the formal commitment that he and his Liberal Cabinet colleagues had made just two years earlier to "take all necessary steps within the jurisdiction of the Parliament of Canada to preserve this [traditional] definition of marriage in Canada." Instead, the Chrétien government capitulated to the courts. Scarcely a month after the *Halpern* ruling, Justice Minister Martin Cauchon introduced a bill on behalf of the government that declared: "1. Marriage, for civil purposes, is the lawful union of two persons to the exclusion of all others. 2. Nothing in this Act affects the freedom of officials of religious groups to refuse to perform marriages that are not in accordance with their religious beliefs." Then, in an extraordinary affront to the dignity of Parliament, the Chrétien government referred the bill to the Supreme Court of Canada for approval prior to passage.

Paul Martin took over as prime minister on 12 December 2003. A few weeks later, on 28 January 2004, his government put an additional question to the Supreme Court of Canada, asking if the centuries-old definition of marriage in the common law as the voluntary union for life of a man and a woman is compatible with the Constitution of Canada. In a unanimous ruling on 9 December 2004, the Court ducked this new question while advising that far from violating the Charter, the government's draft bill on same-sex marriage flowed from the section 15 equality rights that the Court had conferred on homosexuals in the 1995 *Egan* judgment.

With this ruling, the Supreme Court of Canada has all but mandated the imposition of same-sex marriage. Earlier, this same Court legalized abortion on demand in *R. v. Morgentaler*, 1988, and came within one vote of declaring a constitutional right to assisted suicide in *Rodriguez v. British Columbia (Attorney General)*, 1993. The Supreme Court of Canada has had no compunction about invoking the Charter as justification even for imposing amendments to government acts with major spending implications. This process began in *Schachter v. Canada*, 1992, when the Court extended postnatal maternity benefits under the Unemployment Insurance Act to fathers. In *Eldridge v. British Columbia (Attorney General)*, 1997, the Court compelled the Government of British Columbia to introduce free sign-language interpretation in all provincial hospitals. In a unanimous judgment in *Hislop et al. v. Attorney General of Canada*, 2004, the Ontario Court of Appeal amended both the Modernization of Benefits and Obligations Act and the Canada Pension Plan to make survivors' benefits for same-sex common-law couples retroactive to 17 April 1985—the date on which the equality rights provisions of the Charter came into effect. With this ruling, the Court extended survivors' benefits to about 1,500 homosexuals at an estimated cost of $80 million. In *Gosselin v. Quebec (Attorney General)*, 2002, the Supreme Court of Canada came within one vote of ordering the Government of Quebec to hand out extra welfare payments to young Quebecers at an estimated cost to taxpayers of $389 million plus interest.

Ultimately, of course, taxpayers must foot the bills for judicially created entitlements. But that is of no account to our unelected lawmakers in the courts. Time and again, they have ordered governments to spend money on programs that have never been approved by elected representatives of the people in the legislative branch of government. In issuing these orders, these activist judges have repeatedly violated one of the cardinal principles of democracy: no taxation without representation. . . .

A Threat to All Canadians

It bears repeating that the distortion of human rights and fundamental freedoms in the Charter era does not relate just to gays, lesbians, pro-lifers, and traditional Christians. This revolution in the Canadian legal order threatens all Canadians. While theologically orthodox Catholics, Protestants, and Jews are the prime targets for oppression, judges and human rights commissioners have shown that they are prepared to use their enormous powers to harass and coerce any vulnerable minority that defies the orthodoxy of human rights as conceived by these same human rights commissioners and activist judges. Many of the hard-won freedoms of Canadians are fast disappearing. Complacent Canadians should beware. They should remember what happened to complacent Germans in the 1930s. At that time, one of the few Germans who stood up for genuine human rights and fundamental freedoms was Martin Niemoller, a Lutheran pastor and heroic former First World War U-boat captain. For his defiance of [Adolf] Hitler, Niemoller was consigned to the Dachau concentration camp. After the war, he is said to have recalled: "In Germany they came first for the Communists, and I didn't speak up because I wasn't a Communist. Then they came for the Jews, and I didn't speak up because I wasn't a Jew. Then they came for the trade unionists, and I didn't speak up because I wasn't a trade unionist. Then they came for the Catholics, and I didn't speak up because I was a Protestant. Then they came for me, and by that time no one was left to speak up."

> "Since the law must be interpreted before being applied, and since interpretation . . . amounts to shaping the law, judges are condemned to make law whether they want to or not."

Judicial Activism in Canada Is Not a Real Problem

Peter McKnight

Peter McKnight is a columnist and member of the editorial board of the Vancouver Sun *and a legal analyst for Global National. In the following viewpoint, he argues that in Canada the accusation of judicial activism is poorly defined. He points out that Canada is a common-law jurisdiction in which law is based on court precedent; as a result, he says, Canadian judges must make law. In any case, he notes that the Supreme Court of Canada in the vast majority of cases upholds parliamentary laws rather than striking them down. He concludes that the charge of activism has no real meaning.*

As you read, consider the following questions:

1. How did US Supreme Court Justice Potter Stewart define obscenity?

2. How does McKnight say that some academics define judicial activism?

3. How often did Claire L'Heureax-Dubé vote to uphold the law, and why does McKnight suggest this is surprising?

Judicial activism, it seems, is a lot like former U.S. Supreme Court Justice Potter Stewart's notion of pornography.

"I shall not today attempt further to define the kinds of material I understand to be embraced" by obscenity, the learned judge wrote, "but I know it when I see it."

There Is No Definition for "Activism"

Similarly, critics of the Supreme Court of Canada rarely feel the need to define judicial activism, but they know it when they see it. And so great are their powers of perception that they seem to be seeing it more and more frequently.

Indeed, Prime Minister Stephen Harper, whose eyesight is apparently second to none, has made various comments over the years that suggest judges appointed by the former Liberal government do little more than issue activist judgments.

More recently, though, he's tempered his comments somewhat: In response to a reporter's question about whether Canada's judges are activist, Harper responded helpfully, "some are, some aren't."

This, of course, is a completely meaningless comment, and will remain meaningless unless and until Harper defines what he means by "activism." Yet he has thus far failed to provide us with a coherent definition.

Nevertheless, in the lead-up to last Monday's [in March 2006] show trial involving Supreme Court of Canada appointee Marshall Rothstein, Harper did provide us with insight into what he considers the proper role of the judiciary. (Ironically, while the show-and-tell was billed as a forum for acquainting us with Rothstein's judicial philosophy, the whole affair actually told us more about Harper's views.)

Harper informed us that he would choose judges with a "judicial temperament," which "means in my view that when someone's a judge, they're prepared to apply the law rather than make it."

However, since the law must be interpreted before being applied, and since interpretation—determining what the words in a statute mean—amounts to shaping the law, judges are condemned to make law whether they want to or not.

Indeed, in addition to interpreting statutes, judges have "made" whole areas of law, including property law (one of Rothstein's specialties), tort law, contract law and much of family law.

Canada Is a Common-Law Jurisdiction

This might come as a surprise to Stephen Harper, but it shouldn't since Canada (with the exception of Quebec) is a common-law jurisdiction, and "common law" refers to judge-made law, to law based on court precedent.

So in telling us that he will choose judges who apply the law rather than make it, Harper has guaranteed his own failure, since every judge he chooses will inevitably make law. And that leaves us without any definition for "judicial activism," the putative problem Harper seems committed to solving.

To fill this void, many political scientists and some legal academics have offered a different definition, one that doesn't depend on the untenable distinction between making and applying law, but which gives meaning to the concept of judicial activism and allows us to measure it.

According to these academics, judicial activism refers to the tendency of courts to invalidate laws enacted by duly elected legislatures, since doing so ostensibly amounts to courts usurping the role of Parliament. Hence courts that declare many statutes unconstitutional would be considered activist, while courts that refrain from doing so would be said to be exercising judicial restraint.

There is a certain intuitive plausibility to this definition: Court critics usually take umbrage at the thought of unelected judges second-guessing the best-laid plans of Parliament, so courts are usually accused of activism after they invalidate a statute. Further, the definition also seems to be in accord with Harper's statements that courts should defer to the will of Parliament.

Yet the definition isn't entirely satisfactory. After all, since the Constitution is supreme in a constitutional democracy— and it's amazing that many Canadians, including our current prime minister, seem to be unaware of this—it's the duty of the courts to declare unconstitutional statutes that violate the Constitution.

It would therefore be inaccurate to label a court activist simply because it invalidates a law. In a constitutional democracy, we would expect judges who act both judicially and judiciously—that is, those possessed of a "judicial temperament"—to strike down a certain number of statutes.

The all-important question, then, concerns the threshold: How many laws does a court have to invalidate before being considered activist? This is a question that no one has answered, probably because no one can answer it because it all depends on what laws a specific court is considering at a specific time.

In any case, inasmuch as this definition gives an insight into judicial activism, it reveals, that the Supreme Court of Canada—the favourite whipping boy of Stephen Harper and the Conservatives—can hardly be described as activist.

The Supreme Court Is Not Activist

Separate papers by Sujit Choudhry of the University of Toronto faculty of law and Osgoode Hall Law School dean Patrick

Monahan reveal that from 1984 through to 2003, the government won roughly two-thirds of the Charter [referring to the Canadian Charter of Rights and Freedoms] cases that appeared before the court.

In other words, the court only invalidated a law—or granted some other form of relief to rights-seekers—in one-third of cases. The court therefore clearly deferred to Parliament in the vast majority of cases—despite its duty to strike down some legislation—so one can't exactly accuse the court of running roughshod over the intentions of our elected representatives.

Even more surprising is that the judge who was least enthusiastic about invalidating laws is the one Conservatives have most frequently accused of activism.

Monahan looked at the record of each individual judge on the court, and found that former justice Claire L'Heureaux-Dubé—whom Conservatives routinely derided as a "radical feminist," and that's one of the nicer things they had to say about her—would only have granted relief to rights-seekers in 21 per cent of cases, meaning she voted to uphold the law 79 per cent of the time.

There is a fascinating parallel here with the U.S. Supreme Court: According to research by Yale Law School professor Paul Gewirtz, the four members of the conservative wing of that court between 1994 and 2005—Justices Clarence Thomas, Anthony Kennedy, Antonin Scalia and Chief Justice William Rehnquist—were the four judges most likely to strike down U.S. congressional laws.

Thomas, who along with Scalia forms the court's ultra-conservative wing, was most enthusiastic about invalidating laws, voting to do so an astonishing 66 per cent of the time. Scalia, who regularly condemns his colleagues for activism, was close behind, voting the law down in more than 56 per cent of cases.

In contrast, all four members of the liberal wing of the court supported the government in well over half of cases, though they were still more likely to strike down laws than are the judges of the Supreme Court of Canada.

These sobering statistics reveal two things: First, conservative jurists appear much more likely to be activist than liberal ones, if by "activist" we mean possessed of a willingness to frustrate the plans of legislatures. And second, the Supreme Court of Canada appears to be highly deferential to Parliament, despite its responsibility to protect Canadians against the abuse of parliamentary power.

Of course, these statistics won't deter the court bashers— the people who don't need to define activism because they know it when they see it—from accusing the court of usurping the role of Parliament every time the court issues a judgment they don't like.

But the evidence should confirm to everyone else that the court bashers' sound and fury, like their non-definition of "judicial activism," signify nothing.

> *"Government circles say the SC [Su-preme Court] chief justice is trying to impose 'judicial dictatorship' by under-mining the elected parliament."*

Judicial Activism in Pakistan May Lead to Military Intervention

Amir Mir

Amir Mir is a Pakistani journalist who writes for numerous publications. In the following viewpoint, he reports on a struggle between Pakistani president Asif Zardari and Supreme Court chief justice Iftikhar Chaudhry. Zardari elevated two justices to a superior court; Chaudhry rejected the appointments as unconstitutional because he was not consulted. Mir says that the conflict has resulted in a major political crisis. He suggests that Chaudhry is opposing a democratically elected government and expresses concern that the conflict may lead to a military intervention.

As you read, consider the following questions:

1. When, why, and by who was Chief Justice Iftikhar Chaudhry sacked, according to Mir?

2. Who is Nawaz Sharif and who does Mir say he is siding with in the conflict?

3. According to legal experts, who does Mir say should have the ultimate authority in appointing the superior court judges?

A fresh tussle between the Pakistani President Asif Zardari and the Chief Justice Iftikhar Chaudhry over the appointment of the superior court judges has snowballed into a major political crisis which may lead to yet another military intervention by Army Chief General Ashfaq Kayani, who is due to retire this year [2010] and wants his tenure to be extended.

Judicial Dictatorship

Judicial activism seems to be in top gear in Pakistan as the chief justice of the Supreme Court Iftikhar Chaudhry has literally revolted against the president by rejecting his decision to elevate two judges of the Lahore High Court, including the chief justice of the Punjab province despite the fact that they were elevated in accordance with the seniority principle. The chief justice, who was sacked by President [Pervez] Musharraf in 2007 over corruption charges and reinstated by President Zardari in 2009, insists that the president's decision was unconstitutional because he was not consulted as per the law of the land. In a dramatic move in the afterhours on February 13, [2010,] the Supreme Court of Pakistan took suo moto [on its own] notice of the presidential action and suspended the elevation of the two judges by President Asif Zardari.

However, the government circles say the SC [Supreme Court] chief justice is trying to impose "judicial dictatorship" by undermining the elected parliament. They add that Chief Justice Iftikhar Chaudhry had recommended elevation of a junior judge of the Lahore High Court to the Supreme Court while retaining a senior judge, Khawaja Sharif, as chief justice of Lahore High Court. They argue that the chief justice's recommendation was in violation of the apex court's own verdict in 2002 which had set out the principle of seniority for appointment and elevation of the superior court judges. Therefore, they add, the recommendation was rejected by President Zardari.

While the main opposition leader Nawaz Sharif has decided to openly side with the judiciary in the fresh battle between the executive and the judiciary, dubbing the president as the biggest threat to democracy, the government circles say the chief justice has openly declared war against a fragile democracy at the behest of the Pakistan army and the right wing pro-Taliban leaders of the Muslim League. According to Fauzia Wahab, central information secretary of the ruling PPP [Pakistan Peoples Party], the right-wing military-judiciary-opposition parties' axis of evil has taken its dagger out for a final attack on the democratically elected government of the left-wing Pakistan Peoples Party.

The President vs. the Court

However, the federal government intends to challenge the apex court's action. The official circles in Islamabad claim that the chief justice was consulted but his recommendation was rejected by the president because he happens to be the final authority to appoint and elevate judges of superior courts. Yet those close to the chief justice say he is contemplating to initiate contempt of court proceedings against the president and the prime minister from February 18 for overlooking his recommendations for elevation of the two judges who are considered close to Zardari's political rival and opposition leader Nawaz Sharif. Therefore, it is said, the president wanted to get rid of the Lahore High Court's chief justice Khawaja Sharif and therefore elevated him to the apex court. It may be recalled that the majority of judges currently sitting in the Supreme Court and Lahore High Court are of Punjabi origin, most of them are known for their loyalties to right-wing Paki-

Chief Justice Chaudhry and General Musharraf

At that time [2007], General [Pervez] Musharraf perhaps started to realize that the chief justice [Iftikhar Chaudhry] may not support a continuation of his dual role as president and chief of army if a petition was to be filed in the Supreme Court. He filed a reference of misconduct against Justice Chaudhry in the Supreme Court and also made him 'non-functional' on 9 March 2007, without waiting for the decision on the reference. The chief justice was initially placed under house arrest and then assaulted publicly by police. This act evoked countrywide mass demonstrations, rallies and clashes with police and security forces. Since Justice Chaudhry had been transformed into an icon for justice, General Musharraf's popularity and credibility started to tumble within and outside the country. To the general's humiliation, all charges against the chief justice were dropped, and he was unanimously reinstated by a 13-member bench of the Supreme Court on 20 July 2007.

Muhammad Shoaib Butt and Jayatilleke S. Bandara,
Trade Liberization and Regional Disparity in Pakistan,
New York: Routledge, 2009, p. 6.

stan Muslim League and Jamaat-e-Islami; some of them are also known to have a populist anti-West and pro-Taliban inclination.

According to legal experts, the constitutional position pertaining to the elevation of the superior court judges is that the chief justice of the Supreme Court is only a consultee, and it is the president of Pakistan who has the ultimate authority to take a final decision. However, the chief justice, having suspended the presidential orders on February 13, has already constituted a three-member apex court bench which is to decide whether or not the presidential action of February 13 was constitutional. But the chief justice's action of suspending the presidential orders within three hours of their issuance has been described by the PPP circles as a judicial martial law which might eventually pave the way for yet another military intervention by the outgoing Army Chief General Kayani.

> *"Activism on the part of judiciary to come for the rescue of hapless people was a must to bring a meaningful social change [in Pakistan]."*

Judicial Activism Is Needed in Pakistan

Pakistan Press International

Pakistan Press International is Pakistan's independent news agency, founded in 1956. According to the viewpoint, judicial activism is needed in Pakistan to protect the public from profiteers. Justice Nasir Aslam Zahid believes that the judiciary in developing countries like Pakistan needs to do more to facilitate and protect the poor. Strong consumer protection is needed in Pakistan, and judicial activism is the way to achieve such protection.

As you read, consider the following questions:

1. According to the viewpoint, who is Nasir Aslam Zahid?

2. What does Zahid believe to be the root cause of the merciless profiteering in Pakistan?

3. As stated in the viewpoint, what are some of the "real causes" of the "present chaotic situation"?

Pakistan Press International, "Judicial Activism Needed to Protect Consumer Rights," March 29, 2006. Reproduced by permission.

There is a need of a judicial activism to protect the masses, including consumers, from the clutches of merciless profiteers and hoarder Mafia that is presently having a field day, said speakers of the Second Regional Conference on "Building Partnerships for Strong Consumer Protection in South East Asia", organized jointly by the Helpline Trust and Pakistan Certification Bodies Association, here on Wednesday [in March 2006]. Justice (retd [retired]) Nasir Aslam Zahid, addressing the moot, said in Pakistan the real problem was not about making new laws, but implementing the existing laws. He said that we had plenty of good laws, and in fact our constitution was one of the best constitutions of the world, but the real problem was these laws were not being implemented in letter and spirit. He said that unfortunately the rights of consumers were not being safeguarded here. Quoting the examples of unprecedented rise in sugar and oil prices, he said that interests of the poor masses were not being taken care of by the government. He said that the National Accountability Bureau (NAB) first decided to conduct an inquiry into causes of abnormal rise in sugar prices, but later, strangely, it decided not to conduct the probe on the plea that it might further raise sugar prices. He said that not only in sugar industry, but also in all sectors a handful of 'Chaudhries' was busy in the loot and plunder of hapless masses. He said that merciless profiteers and hoarders were sucking the blood of poor masses. He said that prices of almost all commodities were on the rise in Pakistan, and there was no one to halt this malpractice. Justice (retd) Nasir Aslam Zahid said that the root cause of this problem was that our people were not being given the "right of information". He said that the constitution of Pakistan guaranteed the right of expression, of which the right of information was an integral part. He said that unless the right of information was provided to the masses, so that [Pakistanis] could know why and how the things were happening, corruption

Pakistan's National Reconciliation Ordinance

The NRO [National Reconciliation Ordinance] was part of a deal between [General Pervez] Musharraf and the late [former prime minister] Benazir Bhutto whereby Musharraf would remain president while Benazir Bhutto would be allowed to return to Pakistan and participate in politics without facing criminal charges. The NRO put an end to corruption investigations and prosecutions against almost 8,000 individuals—ministers, bureaucrats and politicians. . . .

The NRO was highly controversial and severely criticised by civil libertarians, who argued that the NRO condoned corruption and protected powerful elites by allowing them to avoid accountability for their actions.

Rajshree Jetly,
"Pakistan's Supreme Court and the National
Reconciliation Ordinance: What Now for Pakistan?"
ISAS Brief, no. 147, December 22, 2009.

and cruel price hike would stay. He said that an activism on the part of judiciary to come for the rescue of hapless people was a must to bring a meaningful social change here.

Role of Judiciary in Developing Countries

Giving the example of India, he said that in recent part the Indian judiciary had given many landmark decisions in cases related to the rights of masses. He said that these decisions provided a solid foundation for policy making in India to provide relief to the poor masses. He said that in developed countries the role of judiciary was considered to be limited only to the interpretation of laws, but in the developing countries like Pakistan, the judiciary had to do more for facilitating the poor people. He said that though the legislation was not the job of judiciary, but still it could do a lot to mitigate the sufferings of masses and provide them with badly needed relief, when there were no other avenues left for them. Justice (retd) Nasir Aslam Zahid said that in Pakistan the judicatory had taken notable suo moto [on its own] actions in the cases of kite-flying and serving wedding meals. He urged that citizens and consumer rights' bodies to knock the door of the Supreme Court for all matters related to the fundamental rights of the people, as well as, public interest. He said that the apex court could summon concerned secretaries of government to tell what were the causes of price hike of sugar, oil or other commodities and what the government was doing to safeguard the due rights of citizens.

He said that it was his personal experience that only poor masses were made accountable for the crimes, while the richer classes usually go scot-free. He said that he had been working for prisoner for last couple of years and it was his observation that 99 percent of the prisoners belonged to the poorest of the poor. He said that some 250 women and 500 juvenile prisoners were languishing in the city jails and the majority of them were under-trial prisoners. He said that the conviction ratio of the rape cases in our country was just five percent. He disclosed that our courts during last five years had not decided a signal case of gang rape. He was, however, optimistic the apex court could take suo moto actions to provide the relief to the poor people. He said that laws and courts were there, and all [that was] needed was people and civil society to summon courage and knock their doors against the social injustice and economic cruelties. He said that the civil society could bring a change in Pakistan and it should discharge its due duties in this regard with the renewed sense of responsibility. Justice (retd) M Shaiq Usmani in his presentation on "Consumer policy and law" said that presently in Pakistan the policy was in a state of confusion, while the law was in a state of inertia. He said that the policy was in state of confusion because nobody really knew what to do about consumerism that had hit us recently. He said that protection of the consumer rights in our country was a must because Pakistan was a signatory to the UN [United Nations] Guidelines for Consumer Protection, adopted in 1985. He said that in Pakistan from the very start consumers as an interest group had not been influential because consumers came from every social class and there was no meeting ground between them, and there was also no philosophy or creed to bind them. He said that the labors got their creed in Marxism and Socialism under the *Communist Manifesto*, which gave them the slogan of "Workers of the World Unite". He said that unfortunately there was no such catchy slogan for the consumers. He said that in developed countries responsible governments, strong civil society and consumer rights' bodies had managed to achieve relief for the consumers, but in Pakistan it was considered that consumers were helpless before the capitalists. He said that rampant corruption and bureaucratic sloth had made things worse. He said that the capitalists were feeding us garbage, while service providers in the fields like water and electricity were inefficient. He said that little competition, ineffective press, lack of standardization of goods, and acceptance of poor quality and counterfeit goods by the majority of our consumers due to their poverty were the real causes of the present chaotic situation. Justice (retd) M Shaiq Usmani suggested that strong consumer protection council or similar bodies should be set up all over the country, besides making it sure that existing laws were being properly enforced.

[Datuk] Marimuthu [Nadason], President ERA [Consumer] Malaysia, in his presentation said that in Malaysia prices of 20 essential items including oil and sugar were being controlled by the government, which fully took care of the interests of citizens. He said that utility provider bodies were not free in their country to raise tariff of water, power and gas on their sweet will. He suggested that the consumer bodies should engage their governments as much as they could and build a relation of trust and understanding between them. He said that in the final count it was the consumer himself, which should raise a voice for his rights, as the best consumer protection was the self-protection. Kalyanee Shah, President SEWA Nepal, Javed Jabbar, Mahmood Nanji and others also spoke. Later, the conference adopted the Karachi declaration on consumer protection, aimed at strengthening consumer protection in South Asia and Pacific, consistent with international practices.

Periodical and Internet Sources Bibliography

The following articles have been selected to supplement the diverse views presented in this chapter.

Abhinav Chandrachud	"Dialogic Judicial Activism in India," *Hindu*, July 18, 2009.
Matt Duss	"With Referendum Turkey Becoming Both More Democratic and More Religious," *Think Progress*, September 13, 2010. http://think progress.org.
Stefan Höjelid	"Headscarves, Judicial Activism, and Democracy: The 2007-8 Constitutional Crisis in Turkey," *The European Legacy: Toward New Paradigms*, vol. 15, no. 4, 2010.
James Joyner	"Turning Point in Turkish Democracy," Atlantic Council, September 16, 2010. www.acus.org.
Saban Kardas	"The Turkish Constitutional Court and Civil Liberties," *Today's Zaman*, June 11, 2008.
Ali Khan	"Pakistan's Constitutional Mess," JURIST, October 15, 2007. http://jurist.law.pitt.edu.
LifeSiteNews.com	"'Sex Change' Lunacy and Judicial Activism Cripple Canadian Correction Facilities," October 17, 2005. www.lifesitenews.com.
National Post	"Put Rights Before Constitution," December 5, 2005. www.canada.com/nationalpost.
OnePakistan.com	"No Judicial Activism, Only Judicial Constitutionalism: CJ Iftikhar," October 7, 2010.
Beena Sarwar	"'Judicial Activism' Triggered Emergency," Inter Press Service, November 3, 2007. http://ipsnews.net.

For Further Discussion

Chapter 1

1. Jonathan Witt argues that judicial activism leads to nihilism, while Carson Holloway says judicial activism violates the rule of law. Do you agree that judicial activism over the last several decades has undermined America and resulted in chaos and lawlessness? What examples would you use to defend your opinion?

2. Damon W. Root argues that the Supreme Court should protect individual liberty. Kermit Roosevelt argues that Supreme Court judges should have empathy for the less powerful. In what ways are these views similar? How are they different?

Chapter 2

1. The commerce clause of the Constitution, discussed by Thomas Sowell and Matthew Provance, says that the federal government can regulate trade between states. State governments regulate activity within states themselves. Thus, the commerce clause is about the balance of power between state and federal governments. Are individual liberties necessarily better preserved when state government's have more power? Why or why not?

2. Paul Campos argues that same-sex marriage has no meaningful legal component, and therefore should be decided by political bodies. Is Campos's argument true for Supreme Court decisions on civil rights, such as *Brown v. Board of Education of Topeka*? Why or why not?

Chapter 3

1. Barry Friedman and Jeffrey Rosen argue that judges are reluctant to go against public opinion in major ways. Do you think this is a good thing or a bad thing? In your response, consider the viewpoints by Damon W. Root and Michael Laprarie.

2. In their viewpoint, Wendy Long and Gary Marx claim that polls show Americans are opposed to judicial activism. What would Doug Bandow say is the problem with these polls? Are his arguments reasonable?

Chapter 4

1. Based on the viewpoints by Rory Leishman and Peter McKnight, how are the debates about judicial activism in Canada different than those in the United States? How are they similar?

2. Based on the viewpoint by Pakistan Press International, why might judicial activism be important in countries with authoritarian or semi-authoritarian regimes? In the United States, is judicial activism against authoritarianism unnecessary? Why or why not?

Organizations to Contact

The editors have compiled the following list of organizations concerned with the issues debated in this book. The descriptions are derived from materials provided by the organizations. All have publications or information available for interested readers. The list was compiled on the date of publication of the present volume; names, addresses, phone and fax numbers, and e-mail and Internet addresses may change. Be aware that many organizations take several weeks or longer to respond to inquiries, so allow as much time as possible.

American Bar Association (ABA)
321 North Clark Street, Chicago, IL   60654-7598
(800) 285-2221
e-mail: service@americanbar.org
website: www.americanbar.org

Consisting of more than four hundred thousand legal professionals, the American Bar Association (ABA) is a voluntary organization that provides law school accreditation, continuing legal education, legal analysis and research, programs to assist lawyers and judges in their work, and initiatives to improve the legal system for the public. The ABA's website hosts a wide variety of blogs, including several that focus on the US Supreme Court. It also publishes the *ABA Journal*, a monthly magazine that explores a broad range of legal issues, in addition to a variety of magazines, scholarly journals, and books. The ABA provides frequent analysis of US Supreme Court decisions and other legal issues.

American Civil Liberties Union (ACLU)
125 Broad Street, 18th Floor, New York, NY   10004
(212) 549-2500
website: www.aclu.org

The American Civil Liberties Union (ACLU) is a national organization that works to defend Americans' individual rights
as guaranteed by the US Constitution. The ACLU, with more
than five hundred thousand members and supporters, works
in the courts, communities, and legislatures to preserve civil
liberties. The Supreme Court section of the ACLU website includes summaries of recent civil rights cases heard by the
court as well as articles related to court activities.

American Constitution Society for Law and Policy

1333 H Street NW, 11th Floor, Washington, DC 20005
(202) 393-6181 • fax: (202) 393-6189
e-mail info@ACSLaw.org
website: http://home.acslaw.org/

The American Constitution Society for Law and Policy is a
liberal, progressive organization for legal professionals, with
more than sixteen thousand members. It is dedicated to promoting the vitality of the US Constitution and the fundamental values of equality, justice, and democracy. It shapes legal
debate through conferences, briefings, and lobbying. It also
provides judges, lawyers, and other legal professionals with
opportunities for networking and education. It publishes the
Harvard Law and Policy Review and books such as *Keeping
Faith with the Constitution*. Its website includes *ACS Issue
Briefs*, *ACSBlog*, and numerous articles and guides.

American Enterprise Institute for Public
Policy Research (AEI)

1150 Seventeenth Street NW, Washington, DC 20036
(202) 862-5800 • fax: (202) 862-7177
website: www.aei.org

The American Enterprise Institute for Public Policy Research
(AEI) was founded in 1943 as a private, nonprofit institution
to research matters of public policy and to educate the public
on government, politics, economics, and social welfare. One of
AEI's main activities is to sponsor research and conferences
on topical matters. It also has a website that posts a number

of publications, including commentaries; op-eds; research papers; its monthly newsletter, *AEI Newsletter*; videos and transcripts of its conferences; transcripts of government testimony of its scholars; and schedules of upcoming events. AEI has a publishing division, AEI Press, that has issued a range of books, including many on legal issues.

Cato Institute

1000 Massachusetts Avenue NW
Washington, DC   20001-5403
(202) 842-0200 • fax: (202) 842-3490
website: www.cato.org

Founded in 1977, the Cato Institute is a nonprofit, conservative think tank that provides research and advocates for public policy proposals that support a conservative foreign and domestic agenda. Its main goal is to promote "the promise of political freedom and economic opportunity to those who are still denied it, in our own country and around the world." The organization publishes a number of resources on the US Supreme Court, including the *Cato Supreme Court Review*, which compiles essays from leading conservative constitutional scholars on the most significant court cases of the most recent term. Cato scholars also offer extensive analyses of and commentary on particular legal decisions and relevant Supreme Court issues, as well as a wide range of books on legal, political, and public policy issues.

Center for American Progress (CAP)

1333 H Street NW, 10th Floor, Washington, DC   20005
(202) 682-1611 • fax: (202) 682-1867
e-mail: progress@americanprogress.org
website: www.americanprogress.org

Founded in 2003, the Center for American Progress (CAP) is a progressive think tank that researches, formulates, and advocates for a bold, progressive public policy agenda. Its aim is to restore America's global leadership; develop clean, alternative energies that support a sustainable environment; create economic growth and economic opportunities for all Americans; and advocate for universal health care. CAP scholars provide analyses of significant legal decisions and issues, as well as a wide range of books on legal, political, and public policy issues. The CAP website posts informational videos and video discussions, information on upcoming events, cartoons, interactive maps and quizzes, commentary on topical issues, and a listing of publications by CAP scholars.

The Federalist Society for Law and Public Policy Studies

1015 Eighteenth Street NW, Ste. 425, Washington, DC 20036
(202) 822-8138 • fax: (202) 296-8061
e-mail: info@fed-soc.org
website: www.fed-soc.org

The Federalist Society for Law and Public Policy Studies is a group of more than forty thousand conservative and libertarian legal professionals who advocate for conservative principles. The organization is "founded on the principles that the state exists to preserve freedom, that the separation of governmental powers is central to our Constitution, and that it is emphatically the province and duty of the judiciary to say what the law is, not what it should be." The society's central aim is to sponsor fair, serious, and open debate about the need to enhance individual freedom and emphasize conservative and libertarian values in the American legal system. It offers a number of resources, including a reading list for conservative undergraduate students, studies of the US Supreme Court, and comprehensive analyses of state supreme courts.

Heritage Foundation

214 Massachusetts Avenue NE, Washington, DC 20002-4999
(202) 546-4400 • fax: (202) 546-8328
e-mail: info@heritage.org
website: www.heritage.org

Founded in 1973, the Heritage Foundation was established as a conservative think tank to "formulate and promote conservative public policies based on the principles of free enterprise, limited government, individual freedom, traditional American values, and a strong national defense." Heritage scholars research and formulate public policies to support these goals and then market them to lawmakers and the media in an attempt to shape public opinion on a number of key political, economic, and social issues that affect American life in the twenty-first century. Its website posts commentary, lectures, government testimony by Heritage experts, press releases from the foundation, and listings of upcoming events.

Legal Information Institute (LII)

Cornell Law School, Myron Taylor Hall
Ithaca, NY   14853-4901
(607) 255-1221
e-mail: thomas-bruce@lawschool.cornell.edu
website: www.law.cornell.edu/

The Legal Information Institute (LII) is a nonprofit group that believes everyone should be able to read and understand the laws that govern them, without cost. To make this possible, LII publishes laws online, creates materials that help people understand the laws, and explores new materials to make it easier for people to understand the laws that govern them. Its website includes the text of federal laws, codes, and rules, as well as extensive archives of Supreme Court decisions, opinions, and dissents. It also maintains a regular blog.

Supreme Court of the United States

1 First Street NE, Washington, DC   20543
(202) 479-3000
website: www.supremecourt.gov/Default.aspx

The Supreme Court is the highest court in the United States. Its website includes the Supreme Court *Journal*, which contains the official minutes of Supreme Court deliberations. The site also includes recent court decisions and opinions.

Bibliography of Books

Stephen Breyer   *Making Our Democracy Work: A Judge's View*. New York: Alfred A. Knopf, 2010.

Alex M. Cameron   *Power Without Law: The Supreme Court of Canada, the Marshall Decision, and the Failure of Judicial Activism*. Montreal, Quebec: McGill-Queen's University Press, 2009.

Dan T. Coenen   *Constitutional Law: The Commerce Clause*. New York: Foundation Press, 2004.

Brice Dickson, ed. *Judicial Activism in Common Law Supreme Courts*. New York: Oxford University Press, 2007.

David R. Dow   *America's Prophets: How Judicial Activism Makes America Great*. Westport, CT: Praeger Publishers, 2009.

Ronald Dworkin   *The Supreme Court Phalanx: The Court's New Right-Wing Bloc*. New York: New York Review of Books, 2008.

Barry Friedman   *The Will of the People: How Public Opinion Has Influenced the Supreme Court and Shaped the Meaning of the Constitution*. New York: Farrar, Strauss and Giroux, 2009.

Tom Ginsburg and Tamir Moustafa, eds. — *Rule by Law: The Politics of Courts in Authoritarian Regimes*. New York: Cambridge University Press, 2008.

Kermit L. Hall and James W. Ely Jr., eds. — *The Oxford Guide to United States Supreme Court Decisions*. 2nd ed. New York: Oxford University Press, 2009.

Ran Hirschl — *Towards Juristocracy: The Origins and Consequences of the New Constitutionalism*. Cambridge, MA: Harvard University Press, 2004.

Robert Levy and William Mellor — *The Dirty Dozen: How Twelve Supreme Court Cases Radically Expanded Government and Eroded Freedom*. New York: Sentinel, 2008.

Stefanie A. Lindquist and Frank B. Cross — *Measuring Judicial Activism*. New York: Oxford University Press, 2009.

Thomas R. Marshall — *Public Opinion and the Rehnquist Court*. Albany: State University of New York Press, 2008.

Nathaniel Persily, Jack Citrin, and Patrick J. Egan, eds. — *Public Opinion and Constitutional Controversy*. New York: Oxford University Press, 2008.

Kermit Roosevelt — *The Myth of Judicial Activism: Making Sense of Supreme Court Decisions*. New Haven, CT: Yale University Press, 2006.

S.P. Sathe

Judicial Activism in India: Transgressing Borders and Enforcing Limits. New York: Oxford University Press, 2002.

Antonin Scalia

A Matter of Interpretation: Federal Courts and the Law: An Essay. Princeton, NJ: Princeton University Press, 1998.

Herman Schwartz, ed.

The Rehnquist Court: Judicial Activism on the Right. New York: Hill and Wang, 2002.

Jeff Shesol

Supreme Power: Franklin Roosevelt vs. the Supreme Court. New York: W.W. Norton, 2010.

Index